KINTAIL

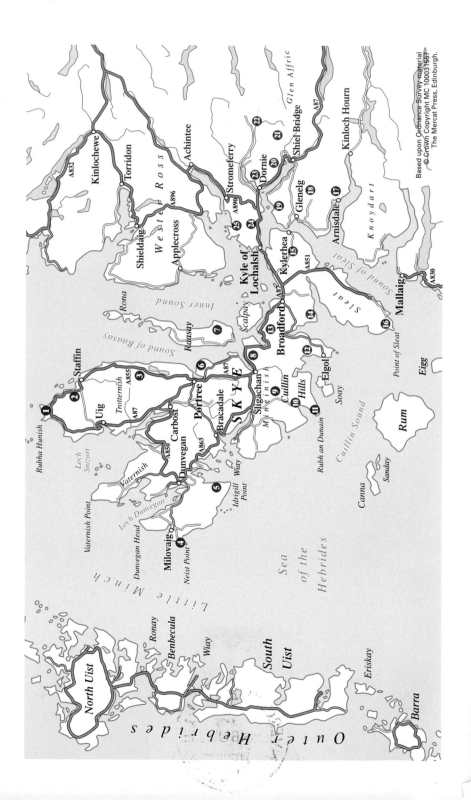

25 WALKS

SKYE AND KINTAIL

Hamish Brown

Series Editor: Roger Smith

914
·115

MERCAT PRESS
EDINBURGH
www.mercatpress.com

Published by
Mercat Press
53 South Bridge
Edinburgh
EH1 1YS

ISBN: 1 841830 070

Main cover illustration: Acairseid an Rubha
Inset: Eilean Donan Castle
All photographs © Hamish Brown, 2000
All maps courtesy of Dave Edwards Cartography, North Berwick

Printed in Spain by Santamaria

CONTENTS

INTRODUCTION

Both Skye and Kintail have their own special identities, historical and geographical, and both yield some of the finest landscapes in the country. There is good walking at any season of the year, which is often enhanced by the proximity of the sea. Some warnings are needed, though.

Those used to walking on clear paths in gentler landscapes may find Skye and Kintail something of a revelation, if not a shock, with a quality of wildness and loneliness that makes it essential to follow sensible procedures. Walks often take longer than expected, so don't be over-ambitious and, if conditions are poor, wait for better weather. Both areas are subject to the vagaries of western weather, but most visits will meet with a mix of good and bad days.

These routes are described for average summer conditions with the ordinary walker in mind, though in winter they can be every bit as rewarding. However, any hill over 610m (2000 ft), in particular, can become a serious undertaking in winter, requiring experience in ice-axe and crampon techniques. It is important to check weather forecasts and be well equipped and provisioned.

Much of the walking, on paths as well as open moorland, can be on the muddy side of wet. Wellingtons are advised for the easier walks and proper boots for the longer and harder routes. Not running into difficulties is important. Sitting down and waiting for mist to clear could lead to starvation; bad as well as good weather can go on for days on end. You should always carry waterproofs and some spare clothes, refreshments, map and compass (and know how to use them). This is not tame country. A walk may be basically easy, like Meall na Suiramach, but it edges huge precipices. Care is vital on all the walks.

While the standard of the walks in this selection, and the demands they make, may vary considerably, none are unduly long or fierce. Major hills like the Black Cuillin or Five Sisters of Kintail are not chosen, being more in the scope of mountaineering. Walking, in the Highlands and Islands especially, is more than just peak-bagging, and the elements of surprise, delight and wonder will be constant rewards for those using this book. Many walks have easier or shorter options and many should not take much more than half a day, so there is always the chance of visiting other places of interest nearby.

Though sparsely populated, all the land is under some form of agricultural use, so it is important not to leave gates open, touch machinery or invade privacy. Dogs are not welcome where there is livestock, and should be strictly under control at all times. Follow the Country Code – and be prepared to talk to local people and other walkers; the background lore can be an enriching part of any area and can only be touched on in this practical outlining. Even the descriptions cannot be as detailed as in gentler country, so a certain self-reliance is demanded of the walker.

The area is rich in wildlife and the sighting of seals or otter, deer or sea eagle can be thrilling. Wildflowers abound still. There is also a tremendous historical, Gaelic background and tradition. If I make Skye and Kintail sound marvellous that is quite reasonable; but it is a flawed perfection with a trio of natural pests to plague the visitor: ticks (in ranker vegetation), clegs (kamikaze horseflies) and the man-eating midges. The only salvation is emigration, and it may be poor comfort to know the biting beasties dislike strong sunshine, high winds and are never found above 10,000 feet.

Enjoy your walks.

Hamish Brown

PRACTICAL INFORMATION

Most of the walks in this book are in areas where there is no restriction on access, but this does not make them rights of way, and where certain warnings are given, these should be heeded. Sheep, often on crofting land, and forestry are commercial enterprises. Many estates offer a positive, year-round welcome to walkers and visitors, but our freedom to roam should always be matched by responsible behaviour. Changes can occur (forests are felled, a new carpark built, etc.), but the general line of the walks should still be clear. Information on changes is welcomed, but while every care has been taken to make descriptions and maps as accurate as possible, the author and publishers can accept no responsibility for error, however caused.

The Ordnance Survey Landranger maps at 1:50,000 cover these Skye and Kintail walks with Sheets 23, *North Skye*; 32, *South Skye*; 33, *Loch Alsh, Glen Shiel*; 24, *Raasay and Loch Torridon*, while Harveys 1:25,000 waterproof Superwalker to Skye is invaluable. These should be used in the field in conjunction with this book. Signposting is limited and paths are often not constructed as such so they can be vague, rough or wet (or icy in winter). Descriptions try to use permanent fixtures and features, but the walker still has to make critical judgements and decisions: for instance, heavy rain can make even small streams dangerous or impassable.

It is as well to leave a note of your plans with someone else. In any emergency simply dial 999 or contact the Portree Police (if on Skye) who will alert the Mountain Rescue Team (tel: 01478 612888). Please note that the reception for mobile phones is still unreliable in the area covered by this book.

Kyle, Broadford and Portree are the main shopping areas with such facilities as banks, chemists, bakers, supermarkets, etc. There are quite extensive bus services (and rail links to Kyle and Mallaig) and a wide range of accommodation: hotels, B&Bs, self-catering, hostels (private and SYHA) and campsites. As these regularly change it is best to obtain current information from the appropriate Tourist Information Centres: Portree, tel: 01478 612137; Broadford, tel: 01478 822361; Kyle of Lochalsh, tel: 01599 534276; Shiel Bridge, tel: 01599 511264. The one in Portree is open all year, the others from April–October.

Though Skye is now bridged to Kyle of Lochalsh, there are useful ferries from Glenelg to Kylerhea and Mallaig to Armadale. They carry vehicles during the summer only but the latter also operates a winter passenger service. Mallaig and Kyle are railway terminals with lines running through majestic scenery and connecting with sleeper services from London to Fort William or Inverness. A car is by no means essential to enjoy Skye and Kintail.

The following are a few books recommended for further reading: T. Marsh, *The Isle of Skye* (1996); A. Nicholson, *History of Skye* (1994); O. Swine, *Skye, The Island and Its Legends* (1973); J. Hunter, *Skye, the Island* (1996). W.H. Murray's *Companion Guide to the West Highlands* (1968) has never been bettered, and the National Trust for Scotland regularly updates its guides to Balmacara and Kintail.

> *Skye I praise for her peace and rest,*
> *The magic views on her ridges,*
> *Heaven sits firm on her rocky hills*
> *And hell is surely her midges.*

Bundalloch Clachan, Loch Long, showing traditional dwellings, 1928
(Copyright: St Andrews University Library)

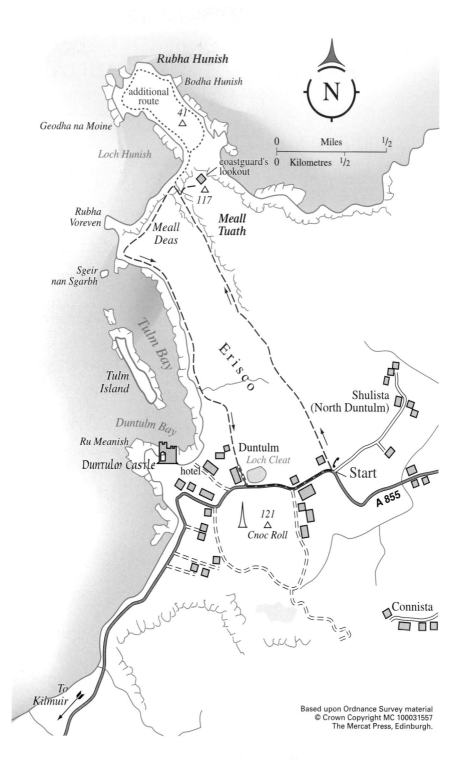

Rubha Hunish

Bodha Hunish

additional route

Geodha na Moine

41
△

Loch Hunish

coastguard's lookout

117
◇ △

Rubha Voreven

Meall Deas

Meall Tuath

Sgeir nan Sgarbh

Tulm Bay

Erisco

Tulm Island

Shulista (North Duntulm)

Duntulm Bay

Ru Meanish

Duntulm Castle

hotel

Duntulm

Loch Cleat

Start

A 855

121
△
Cnoc Roll

Connista

To Kilmuir

N

0   Miles   ¹/₂
0   Kilometres   ¹/₂

SKYE'S NORTHERN EXTREMITY (MEALL TUATH & RUBHA HUNISH)

Trotternish, the winged peninsula, running north like a decayed spine, has contrasting east and west faces. The east presents a great cliff-edge and landslip features, with many sea-touching verticalities, while the west offers convex hills and a wide apron of scruffy moorland. Both sides have scattered crofting communities and associations with Flora MacDonald and Bonnie Prince Charlie. An anti-clockwise drive can easily take in this walk and other features like Duntulm Castle and the Folk Museum at Kilmuir. There is limited parking at the start, so be careful not to block any access.

Rubha Hunish is Skye's most northerly point; a hidden promontory guarded by spectacular cliffs and only reached by an exposed path which is not for the timid. However, it is only an option, and the finest views are from the coastguard's lookout hut on top of Meall Tuath – an easy walk across the moors. As may be guessed, the sunsets are quite stunning and there is time enough to watch sun kiss sea (or Hebrides) and still walk out back to the start.

Cross the gate beside the telephone box (GR 423743; see Information) and pass right of the sheep fank and up on to the heathery bank. Looking ahead, you can just make out the coastguard's lookout building on top of Meall Tuath. Left of this is a marked dip and then the lesser height of Meall Deas. The walk – by a variety of sheep tracks rather than a clear path – heads for the dip, visits Meall Tuath then crosses the dip to Meall Deas and descends to return by the shore of Duntulm Bay with Tulm Island anchored to westwards – a straightforward-enough circuit.

INFORMATION

Distance: 7km (4.5 miles).

Maps: Landranger 23

Start and finish: By telephone box/minor road to North Duntulm (Shulista), 800m (° mile) east of Duntulm Hotel. Sheep fank and signpost (GR 423743). (Alternative parking at the hotel or Duntulm Castle parking area.)

Terrain: Moorland sheep tracks or open ground. Parts can be wet. The point itself is reached by an exposed path. Cliffs: care needed.

Toilets and refreshments: Duntulm Castle Hotel (summer only).

Opening hours: Duntulm Castle – open access. Skye Museum of Island Life, Kilmuir: Mon–Sat, 0900–1730. Tel. 01470 552279.

The cliffs of Rubha Hunish

Keep on the high ground. The slopes above Tulm Bay mark the old crofting clachan of Erisco, with the ruins of well-spaced and well-built houses. Where the fence – which comes up from the north end of the bay – crosses an overgrown wall, there is a stile. A clearer path leads on into that gap: a long, shallow valley that is often a bit boggy, with the best going being on the right flank. When followed to its end there is a startling revelation of sheer cliffs, quite invisible till then, with the grassy world of Rubha Hunish stretching out below, seemingly quite beyond reach, though it is from here that the 'easy' access lies (see below).

The old coastguard lookout on top of the Meall Tuath cliffs

Backtrack to the first easy line up on to Meall Tuath to reach the dramatically sited old coastguard's look-out post, a blessed shelter if windy or wet. The cliffs are 117m (380 ft) high and range east and west in vertical basaltic columns, so great care should be taken, especially if there are children present. This walk, for both safety and enjoyment, should be reserved for a calm, clear day. The view is splendid with the Shiants bold and the Outer Hebrides ranged beyond a scattering of nearer islands, the big hills of Harris being notable. East lies the mainland with the hills of Torridon on parade.

Use sheep tracks to return to the gap. Walk up Meall Deas and then curve round and down to Duntulm Bay, crossing the fence near the sea by a stile made of a fish box. Walk towards the jagged castle ruin on its prow. As you draw level with the south end of the island, contour up to the top of the field wall and, when it turns right, do likewise, along to a gate of sorts (with a stile to the left) and then continue by the wall. Go through a gate in the wall to reach the drive out to the A855 by the white, identikit buildings, at one time the coastguard's accommodation. Loch Cleat lies on the left.

The optional extra of exploring Rubha Hunish is more fearsome in prospect than practice, but has obvious dangers and should not be undertaken in adverse conditions. From the gap between the Mealls there is a path, improbable as this may seem at first glance, starting at a prominent boulder tight against the edge on the Meall Deas side, initially no more than a rocky gully then winding along and down under the sheer cliffs topped by the lookout. It can be studied from the boulder before any commitment is made. The rock can be greasy when damp.

Rubha Hunish is worth circuiting. The east cliffs hold the main features of stacks, natural arches and all manner of weird rocks. All the stacks have been climbed within the last decade and abseil slings left behind may be spotted. Looking back, or on the return, the amazing feel of the place is emphasised by the pleated miles of cliff that isolates this pasture. Sheep graze it still and the stripes of 'lazy-bed' cultivation remain. There are several climbing routes on the wall of cliffs, one with the name *Minch an' Tatties*.

Before leaving the area have a look at Duntulm Castle, a cluster of rotten fangs of masonry on a broken face of cliff-girt promontory. It must have been a formidable bastion at one time, a Macdonald castle dating to the days of James VI and I. There's a cairn in memory of the Macarthurs who were the hereditary pipers to the Lords of the Isles. A Gaelic couplet translates: 'The world will end /But love and music will endure'. A rope-edged path leads round and down to the shore then a track from a slip (impassable at high tide) takes you up to the hotel.

Based upon Ordnance Survey material
© Crown Copyright MC 100031557
The Mercat Press, Edinburgh.

THE WEIRD WORLD OF THE QUIRAING

Towards the north end of the Trotternish peninsula lies an area of weird and wonderful landscape where the lava mountains have been split and separated into endless bumps and hollows, crags and pinnacles, all weathered and sculpted over the centuries. The most spectacular area, the Quiraing, lies tight under Meall na Suiramach, 543m (1768 ft).

Access is by a small road that crosses from Staffin to Uig by the 250m (815ft) Bealach Ollasgairte – not named on the map – where there is a small carpark (bealach means *pass*). Be there early to ensure a parking place.

From the carpark, the view north-east leads the eye to a natural gap with the bulk of the Prison sticking up to the right. A footpath makes a traverse of character to reach the gap between the Prison and the cliffs. The slopes below the traverse are unusually green from the rich basalt rocks. The view southwards is outstanding, especially in early-morning light.

Continue to the cairned pass between the Prison and the wild landscape facing it, dominated by the pinnacle called the Needle. The main walk continues to contour along the cliffs, but the Needle and other features in the chaos above offer a unique experience for those who don't mind very steep slopes. Two hours can be spent very easily up in that weird world, a place more of Bram Stoker than C.S. Lewis.

There are many alternative paths now, so a detailed description is given. Climb up steeply and then move right to pass

INFORMATION

Distance: 7km (4.5 miles)

Map: Landranger 23.

Start and finish: Small parking area at top of the pass on the Staffin to Uig mountain road (GR 440679).

Terrain: Mainly clear paths, but some extremely steep slopes. Cliffs: care needed. The expedition is not advised during wet or cloudy conditions.

Toilets and refreshments: None. Nearest village, Uig (7km).

The weird and wonderful Quiraing landscape

The sun reveals the beauty of the cliffs

behind the Needle. (This feature has been climbed but, as the guidebook says, the fact is recorded more as a warning than a recommendation.) Beyond the Needle the path forks. Take the right variant (the descent uses the other) to go over to a deep gash between soaring rocks then scrabble up this to reach a hidden hollow.

A path can be seen working up the grassy slope ahead, dominated by a sharp pinnacle on the right. Take this path, and at pinnacle level you are faced with the side of the Table. Move rightwards towards where a small pinnacle lies between two huge skyscraper-like blocks and find a path facing this, which curls up on to the flat world of the Table. (The Table can also be reached by moving left and circling round and up to where the Table abuts against the final wall of cliff.)

The Table is a remarkably flat, round, grassy area. Anciently, cattle were brought up to this fastness for security against raiders. Walk round it and climb up to the north-west, where a Side Table below the cliffs gives a view down over all. Paths, tight along under the cliffs to the south, lead to a gap where another pot-holed tower can be ascended – a further extra-ordinary viewpoint. There is a certain frustration that no route up on to Meall na Suiramach exists: the top cliff is an effective barrier which, eventually, you will look down from.

Legend has it that a smith herding on the Quiraing found a strange keyhole on a rocky wall. He made an impression and, with the key thus made, forced his way into a cavern where the Fianna warriors lay asleep. Having half-roused them by blowing Fionn's whistle, he ran in terror from their wild appearance. He locked the door and threw the key in a loch, still called locally *the loch of the smith's rock*.

Heading downwards, there is a confusion of paths,

but once below the circling wall of the Table aim for the paths (a bit right) that twist *up* to a gap. From this gap there is a last view back to the lost world of the Table and, on the other side, you look directly down on the Needle. The path down from the gap leads to the original junction, and thereafter you reverse the outward route to pass the Needle and descend the skirts of grass to the col with the Prison.

Continuing the walk northwards, the path soon crosses a fence line to lead on to a strange, hollow land lying below the big cliffs and further shattered prows, pinnacles and peaks to seawards. A lochan is passed, and when the battlemented landscape at the far end nears, a man-made wall linking the gaps is reached. Beyond, the path angles up on to the ridge (cairn), where there is a view over the north end of Skye (Walk 1) to the Minch and the Outer Hebrides.

The large Coire Mhic Eachainn bites back at your feet; turn left to walk up the ridge between the corrie and the Quiraing cliff line. You break up on to the upper, grassy slopes of Meall na Suiramach, but follow the cliff line to a cairn on a flat area – where you can look down on the Table etc. – then turn west along traces of path to reach the trig pillar at the summit of the hill. This flattish, featureless summit is not advisable in mist.

The strange rock formations of the Quiraing

The view eastwards ranges from Torridon to Cape Wrath and encompasses many notable mountains, while much of Skye is in view. Relish the prospect then head off south-west to pick up a line of poles. Once the angle steepens, bear off left for a steep, though straightforward, descent back to the carpark.

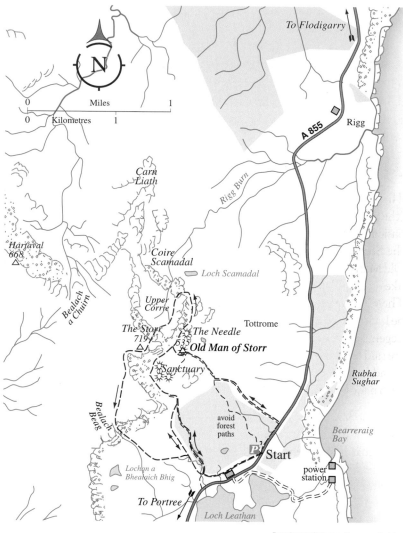

To Flodigarry

N

0   Miles   1

0   Kilometres   1

A 855   Rigg

Carn
Liath

Rigg Burn

Hartaval
668

Coire
Scamadal

Loch Scamadal

Bealach
a Churn

Upper
Corrie

Tottrome

The Storr   The Needle
719   535
Old Man of Storr

Sanctuary

Rubha
Sughar

Bealach
Beag

avoid
forest
paths

Bearreraig
Bay

Lochan a
Bhealaich Bhig

P Start

power
station

To Portree

Loch Leathan

Based upon Ordnance Survey material
© Crown Copyright MC 100031557
The Mercat Press, Edinburgh.

THE OLD MAN OF STORR

The Storr, with its Sanctuary pinnacles, is one of Britain's most extraordinary natural features and, as such, is a popular excursion for many who would not normally tackle such a demanding walk. Parking is limited and apt to be crowded in the tourist season, so an early start is advisable. While most visitors simply climb to the Sanctuary to see the Old Man and return, it is possible to reach the summit of the Storr itself, given the right conditions.

The A855 north from Portree passes Loch Fada (the *long loch*) and Loch Leathan (the *wide loch*), basically one loch, with the cliffs and pinnacles of the Storr dominating the view, in particular the Old Man of Storr – the leaning pinnacle that looks like one of Obelix's menhirs in the *Asterix* books. The Old Man was once higher, but not only has he lost his head but also a 'wife' pinnacle has fallen. Legends gather round these figures, of course: they are said to be the petrified forms of a couple fleeing invaders whose leader could turn men to stone with a look of his one eye.

The wood by the carpark is gradually being made more user-friendly. At present, however, the path up through it (from a roofed stile) is just too boggy to be practical. Most people follow a path to the left (Portree side), which runs up inside the left edge of the wood, or walk along the A855 to a gate at the north edge of the wood and then up outside the wood. These options are also boggy in places.

Follow one of these alternative paths (until remedial work

INFORMATION

Distance: Sanctuary visit only: 4.5km (3 miles). The Storr Traverse: 8km (5 miles).

Map: Landranger 23.

Start and finish: Carpark, by wood, 10km north of Portree on A855 (GR 507526).

Terrain: Paths or open hillside with some very steep ground. Some boggy areas. Cliffs: care needed.

Toilets and refreshments: None. Portree (10km) nearest facilities.

Storr from the south

produces a permanent route) up to the aptly named Sanctuary, an unreal and atmospheric place of geological wonder. The sheer cliffs backing the site soar 200m (over 600 ft) in blank walls and deep clefts, while the floral, green slopes (loved by rabbits) are dotted with pinnacles with names like the Needle, with its twin eyes, and the 50m (165 ft) Old Man – the bulbous megalith first climbed by Don Whillans in 1955. The Old Man's 'head' fell off in a severe storm over a century ago.

This area is akin to Ben Tianavaig (Walk 6) and the Quiraing (Walk 2) in being a dramatic landslip feature. The overlying volcanic mass of rock caused the underlying sediments to slide down with a cataclysmic tearing apart of the rocks, some of which have weathered into peculiar features such as the Storr Rocks.

The Storr itself, the hill, is 719m (2358 ft) and is a splendid viewpoint, being the highest summit in

northern Skye. It is best tackled by the more experienced walker, unless in clear, windless, settled weather. From the Needle in the Sanctuary, follow a path northwards below the cliffs till it is possible to break up on to the easier ground of Coire Scamadal. Walk up to an obvious break in the headwall crags. The route is cairned in places.

The Old Man of Storr

You land on the tilted plateau not far from the summit trig pillar, which perches on the edge of the fearsome eastern cliffs.

Given plenty of time, a complex and rough descent can be made via the shambolically rocky Carn Liath spur to the north (joining the A855 some miles north of the start), but this is best left to the experienced: route-finding is difficult. (There is good climbing on the dolerite rock.) The easiest option – other than returning by the ascent route – is to walk south from the summit down the green-tilted slope to the first obvious col, the Bealach Beag, and then follow the burn down from it for a while (care required) before angling back towards the plantation and carpark.

There's a true story concerning these Storr lochs and the fugitive Prince Charlie who was hiding on Skye. It was thought he was in danger and should move to Raasay, but every boat was guarded or commandeered and the task looked hopeless. The young laird of Raasay and his brother (still recovering from a wound) remembered a rowing boat on these lochs and took it – manhandling it down to the sea and rowing to Raasay for a bigger boat in which they gave the prince passage.

It is worth walking out to the cliff edge both to fully grasp what a feat this was and to see what there is there today – a small power-station, fed by a pipe from the lochs and reached down a seemingly endless flight of steps. On the shore below the Storr a hoard of coins was found (a Viking pile?) in 1891, and among brooches, bracelets and rings were scores of Anglo-Saxon silver coins – and 18 coins minted in distant Samarkand.

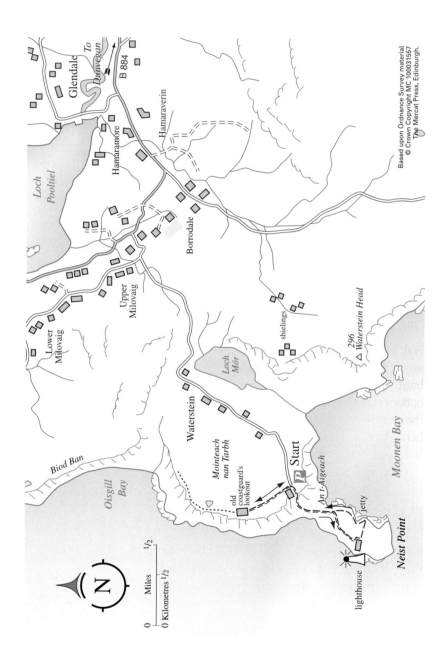

Based upon Ordnance Survey material
© Crown Copyright MC 100031557
The Mercat Press, Edinburgh.

NEIST POINT

INFORMATION

Distance: 11km (7 miles).

Map: Landranger 23.

Start and finish: Small parking area at end of public road leading to the lighthouse (GR 133477).

Terrain: Paths and open moorland, some steep ground. Cliffs: care needed.

Toilets and refreshments: Possibly at the lighthouse or in Glendale (5km), summer only.

Opening hours: Dunvegan Castle: Easter–October, open daily. Other museums etc., tend to be closed on Sunday.

Note: Please do not take dogs on this walk.

Neist Point is the most westerly land in Skye so, not surprisingly, offers good views. The name is tautological as Neist is Norse for *Point*. This arm reaches out into the Minch, ending in a hand, curved as if trying to grab the rushing tides – a most evocative spot. More prosaically, the lighthouse is the objective for many tourists, so it is advisable to arrive early as parking is limited – or leave it till late in the day in the hope of a Hebridean sunset.

The last motoring mile takes you through the hamlet of Waterstein with Loch Mor below, backed by the bold bulk of Waterstein Head. The lighthouse is well signposted from the Glendale approach. The concrete path to the lighthouse comes as quite a surprise. Note that dogs are banned from the area.

A flight of steps plunges down the cliffs and there is an overhead cable for winching supplies, or tourists' baggage if staying at any of the accommodation options at the lighthouse, itself not generally open to the public – although there is sometimes a tea-room here. All is as white and trim as you expect. The far horizon is rimmed with the Outer Hebrides across the Minch while Waterstein Head, 296m (962 ft), the highest of the Duirinish cliffs, dominates across Moonen Bay. The lighthouse was built in 1908 and became automatic in 1989.

Once down the steps the path runs on to round the half-cone of An t-Aigeach, *the Stallion's Head*, which makes a fine viewing point (but not during nesting time). Off-season you may see rock-climbers on the cliffs. A climb called *Supercharger* goes up the centre of the An t-Aigeach 105m (350

Waterstein Head

The lighthouse on Neist Point

ft) cliffs. All the resident seabirds seem to be here; look out for the reintroduced sea-eagle and for the rafts of shearwater out on the sea.

Seals are often seen and basking sharks or killer whales may be spotted. There may be more shelter down by the small jetty, and you can spend a lot of time just exploring without too much effort – but great care is essential, especially with children in a party. Neist Point can be a windy spot, so wrap up well for the walk and any exploration.

Just before reaching the lighthouse there is a small graveyard that appeared almost overnight. It was built as a set for the film *Breaking the Waves*, which went on to win the Silver Medal at the 1996 Cannes Film Festival. It is all fake; the 'stones' are fibreglass!

There is no return to the start except up the steps. After that effort, a recommended route is to head left up a small track and continuing paths to reach an old coastguard lookout site, which gives perhaps the most fascinating view of the lighthouse. North can be seen the huge, vertical cliffs above Oisgill Bay: the Biod Ban. (Biod an Athair, 8km north again, is the highest sea-cliff on Skye.) Return to the start or explore on a bit if the lure of changing sea and chancy views is not yet satisfied.

Glendale has a small store and a café that, if open, serves huge portions of sinful cake. On the road over to Loch Dunvegan (at GR 197497) there is a monument to the Glendale Martyrs: in 1882 local crofters (and the minister, for once) were in the forefront of resistance to the landlord's effort to clear the population. The London government sent a gunboat to Loch Pooltiel! Some of the 'rebels' were jailed and the event was one of several in Skye that brought the disgraceful exploitation of the people to public knowledge and led to reforms.

Dunvegan Castle, the seat of Clan Macleod and Skye's most famous tourist objective, can easily be combined with a visit to Neist Point. As well as the historic castle, there are gardens, a craft shop, a restaurant and boat trips to view seals in the loch. In Dunvegan, too, is the Giant Angus MacAskill Museum, with a life-size model of this huge figure – all 7 ft 9 in (236 cm) of him. Between Dunvegan and Neist Point is the Colbost Croft Museum showing how people lived on the land in the nineteenth century.

Sunset by Neist Point

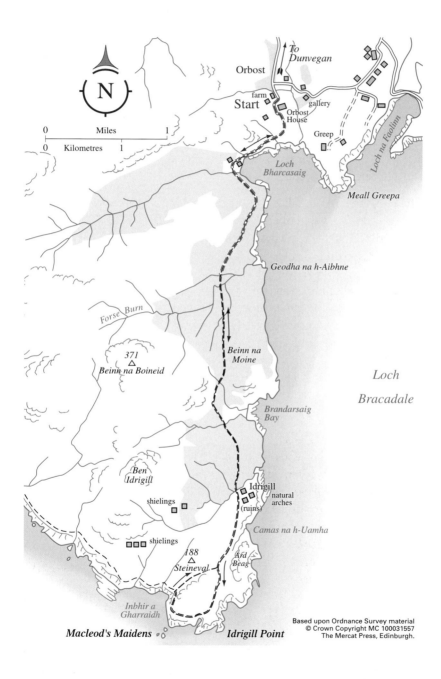

IDRIGILL POINT AND MACLEOD'S MAIDENS

The sea cliffs of Duirinish are among the most impressive on Skye; there are an incredible number of natural arches, stacks, caves and other features. The walk out to Idrigill Point gives both an excellent expedition and a selection of fascinating features, the finest being the three sea-pinnacles of Macleod's Maidens. It is worth keeping for a fine day and the going is quite strenuous, even if pathed.

The remoteness of Idrigill is seen in it twice being used as a safe place to hide the half-mad Lady Grange who had been abducted when she threatened to expose her husband's Jacobite plotting. (He was the brother of Mar, who led the 1715 rising.) Everyone was told that she had died and a 'funeral' was held in Edinburgh – meanwhile she was secretly carried off to Idrigill. She was shunted about to Heisker, St Kilda (for 7 years!), Assynt and other lonely places. When she did die, there was another fake funeral in Duirinish while her body was buried quietly at Trumpan.

From the start an excellent farm/forestry track skirts Orbost House and runs along above Loch Bharcasaig with views out over Loch Bracadale to Harlosh Island and the Minginish coast. The track then enters mature conifer woodland that rather limits the views till you come out to cross a stream, the Forse Burn, with the new plantings ahead still too low to cut off the sea views. The track stops but the path remains clear (some cairns or markers) and climbs steadily to reach a small pass, marked by a cairn (Beinn na Moine to the east).

Beyond lies the big basin draining to Bharcasaig Bay, and this has to be crossed. The path initially

INFORMATION

Distance: 16km (10 miles).

Map: Landranger 23.

Start and finish: Orbost. On unclassified road off the Dunvegan–Broadford A863 road. Park at/near the farm (B&B) but do not block access (GR 256434).

Terrain: Forest tracks and open hillside paths. Cliffs: care needed.

Toilets and refreshments: None. Dunvegan (5km) nearest facilities.

Bharcasaig Bay

keeps by the top fence (crossing it twice) and then swoops down to a small sheep fank and crosses the burn to climb up the far slope. When the path descends to the next stream, there is a kissing gate to mark the end of the plantings. The grass is *machair* – firm and bright with daisies, buttercups, self-heal and eyebright.

The path now aims for a tight, narrow valley that runs between Ard Beag (to seaward) and Steinaval. The route goes through this pass, but it is worth diverting to gain the northern ridge of Ard Beag where there is a view down to the cliff-girt bay of aptly-named Camas na h-Uamha (*strand of the cave*), beyond which is a remarkable and unusual pair of natural arches. Either return to the path or contour along the Ard Beag flank of the pass to descend to the far end of the valley where it twists left.

There are sheep trails everywhere, but the path keeps high to head on along the same line, above some green flats and then an area of knolls. A cairn on the cliff edge is positioned right above the Maidens, but you can gain the edge further west. The sudden appearance of the three stacks is a memorable shock: the tall, head-bent, mother figure is about 65m (210 ft) and beyond her are two contrastingly shaped daughter pinnacles.

Macleod's Maidens

The Maidens, not surprisingly, are surrounded in hoary legends. The Valkyries, for instance, were seen on Healaval weaving a web of death before the battle of Clontarf (AD 1014) that saw the Norsemen defeated. Another story suggests the name arose after the wife and two daughters of the fourth Chief of Clan Macleod drifted across the Minch to be wrecked here.

Do wander westwards along the cliff (with care, the top is exposed and crumbly) to gain the green pastures above the next bay, Inbhir a' Gharraidh, beyond which are massive vertical cliffs. As well as the flowers mentioned above there are tormentil, thyme and bell heather. The Maidens are seen in profile.

Natural arches on the way to Idrigill Point

You can either retrace your steps or, from this green area, cut through to the north-east by a small, shallow valley to drop into the Steinaval–Ard Beag pass at its southern end. Thereafter the outward route is simply reversed. If you turn first right driving away from Orbost (Roag road) the first building met is the woodcut workshop and gallery of Paul Kershaw, who produces marvellously detailed pictures of Skye and its scenery. Thanks to the Clearances, there's an Orbost by the Snowy River in Australia.

Otta Swire's book, long overdue a reprint, has a judgement-of-Solomon story attached to this area. A Macleod's cow fell off the cliff and landed on another Macleod's fishing boat, smashing it and breaking the beast's neck. There was a great row, as first one Macleod claimed the other's boat had killed his cow, while the other counter-claimed that the cow smashed his boat and ruined him. They took the case to their chief who had as his guest the chief of Macdonald and he was asked, as a neutral, to make the judgement.

'If the cow hadn't fallen the boat would not have been damaged,' the visitor mused and the fisherman grinned, 'But if the boat had not been under the cliff the cow might not have been killed.' The other smiled in turn. 'If the cliff had not been there, none of this would have happened. The cliff is to blame and the owner must compensate with both a cow and a boat,' and he sat back smiling in turn while everyone laughed, including the Macleod chief who would have to make the restitution.

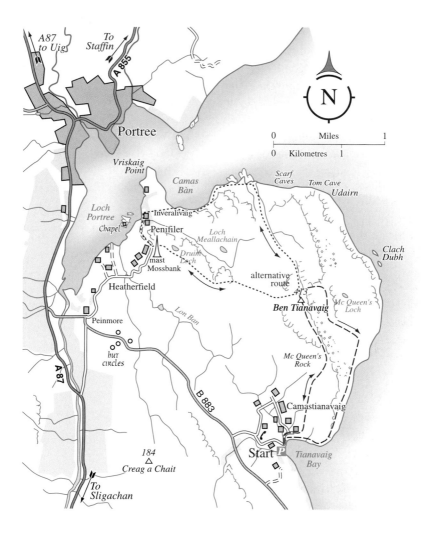

HALF A HILL: BEN TIANAVAIG

Though only half a hill, this delightful oddity offers many options: the walking is clean and kindly (by Skye standards) and you can ascend from the north, Penifiler, or the south, Camastianavaig, equally easily, combine them or make other circuits. Though only a modest 413m (1355 ft) the summit view is one of the best in Skye, with Raasay close-anchored by, the ranges of the Black and Red Cuillin jagging and rolling to the south and the Old Man of Storr catching the eye north over Portree.

Ben Tianavaig is the lowly triangle of hill backing the view out over Portree harbour, but is strangely neglected by walkers. The eastern slopes have pulled off in the sort of landslip seen on the Storr and Quiraing, so it has the same strange atmosphere, if not on such a scale. Perhaps you should climb this peak first as an introduction to the area's geological impressiveness. It really is only half a hill, and the brown moorland skirts seen as you drive between Portree and Sligachan don't even hint at the green weave overlooking the Sound of Raasay.

My favourite route starts and finishes at Tianavaig Bay, and is described first. Turn off the A87 Sligachan–Portree road where signposted for Braes then, after 3km (2 miles), turn left on to the Camastianavaig road. Take the right fork at the telephone box to twist down to the bay, where you can park by some picnic tables. Camas means *bay* and Tianavaig (Chee-an-avaig) is *the bay's stormy top*, but it is a sheltered corner in many ways, with the old and new white houses running along below the slopes of the hill.

INFORMATION

Distance: 6.5km (4 miles).

Map: Landranger 23.

Start and finish: By shore of Tianavaig Bay (GR 508389). Take the B883 turn-off from the A87 leaving Portree and follow Camastianavaig sign. Right fork at telephone box.

Terrain: Unusually dry, easy walking, open hillsides with sheep paths. Cliffs: care needed.

Toilets and refreshments: None. Portree (7km) nearest facilities.

Ben Tianavaig from the south

Head up towards the hamlet, briefly: the road makes an initial S-bend, and as it swings left there is a post-box and a gated track (on the right) leading to a couple of houses. Turn off just before this gate to go up between a fir plantation (left) and a bungalow, follow this break to a not-too-obvious gap in the field boundary and so gain the open moorland. Turn left and use sheep tracks to make a steep, rising traverse, skirting a band of crags, beyond which the view of the hill opens out.

Ben Tianavaig from Portree

On the skyline there is a distinctive wart-like bump. Aim somewhat left of this and simply pick the best way to gain height easily. The ground becomes dry and the walking pleasant, with a sudden revelation when the ridge proper is reached: the east is bounded by striated precipices and steep, green flanks, with the rended hollows and towers of the landslip plain to see. Dun Caan (Walk 7) looks almost within touching distance and there's a glimpse north to the Old Man of Storr. Continue on close-cropped grass up to the slender trig pillar on the summit where the panorama can best be enjoyed. From this impressive vantage point, Portree sprawls inland from its harbour (the name is Gaelic for *bay of the hill*). More romantically, the summit is a traditional burial place of Diarmid and Grainne.

Whatever descent route you use, it is worth studying the lie of the land from on high. Note how not far down northwards the green hollow below the east face runs up to a ridge abutting the main crest. This is the best choice. Turn off to gain the head of this steep valley that can simply be followed down to the coast but, better, swing left (east) to follow the outer rim of this rabbit-favoured hollow and descend on the ridge itself. There is no path but plenty of useful sheep tracks, and you can wind along to suit your curiosity. Small pinnacles and towers make contrasting foregrounds for Dun Caan. The going is steep – sometimes very steep – but firm underfoot. Drop right down to the vivid-green arc of pasture by the shore.

From there, a good sheep track heads southwards to return to Tianavaig Bay. At the spot where the cliffs press down to the sea there is just room for the path and no more. The going round the bay is a bit wet (through birch scrub) but you can cut across the shore a bit, or contour higher to regain the start of the walk where it joins the open moor.

If this return appears intimidatingly steep, you can return by the pleasant ascent line or go down the north ridge to where the angle eases and then use good sheep tracks to traverse 'home' along the west flank. The other option is to head right down northwards, aiming for either Camas Ban or, more directly, to the radio mast at Penifiler, keeping above the crag line by the secretive Druim Loch. If you are being met at Penifiler, the driver should park 150m back from the turning place and be careful not to block any local access. A sign on the gate advises that 'Dogs are forbidden'.

If ascending from Penifiler, the road approach from the A87 is initially the same but then the Penifiler signs are followed for a twisty mile. The track onwards for Vriskaig Point and Camas Ban (*Fair Bay*) is pleasant and the cliffs beyond are fine. At the latest, head up by the parallel streams for Ben

Silhouettes and gathering clouds

Tianavaig, the last easy break in the crags – the Scarf Caves etc., are not accessible for walkers. The going becomes easier as height is gained. Half a hill will prove better than some complete hills.

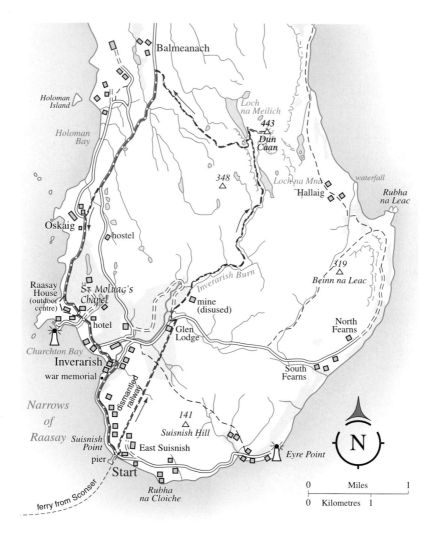

Balmeanach

Holoman
Island

Loch
na Meilich

443
△
Dun
Caan

Holoman
Bay

348
△

Loch na Mna   waterfall

Hallaig

Rubha
na Leac

Oskaig

hostel

Inverarish Burn

319
△
Beinn na Leac

Raasay
House
(outdoor
centre)

St Moluag's
Chapel

mine
(disused)

North
Fearns

hotel

Glen
Lodge

Churchton Bay

Inverarish

war memorial

South
Fearns

Narrows
of
Raasay

dismantled
railway

141
△
Suisnish Hill

Suisnish
Point

East Suisnish

Eyre Point

pier

Start

N

Rubha
na Cloiche

| 0 | Miles | 1 |
| 0 | Kilometres | 1 |

ferry from Sconser

Based upon Ordnance Survey material
© Crown Copyright MC 100031557
The Mercat Press, Edinburgh.

DUN CAAN OF RAASAY

In 1773, James Boswell danced a reel with a local girl on top of Dun Caan, the climax of an historic visit to the island with the redoubtable Dr Johnson. Visitors have been raving about Raasay ever since. Compelled to choose just one walk from the twenty-five, this could well be the connoisseur's choice: the setting of Raasay is superb, it has a charm all of its own and, in Dun Caan, one of the most recognisable summits, full of character and with outstanding views.

Dun Caan is visible from many places on the western mainland as well as from Skye. Walk 6, Ben Tianavaig, faces it across the sound. Raasay has so much to offer that staying for several days is recommended. There is a welcoming hotel and an outdoor centre offering cycle hire, camping, courses, walks etc.

Geologically, Raasay belongs to the mainland, and this narrow sound between it and Skye is a glacier-gouged trench, 500m deep in places. Old iron works are much in evidence on landing. There is a dismantled railway incline running straight up the hill: take this rather unusual 'path', which is steep initially through the ruins of the mine workings then clear ahead, with a sighting of Dun Caan. Inverarish, the white church and other buildings round the bay can be seen, sheltered below extensive woodlands; an attractive corner.

The line enters the forest (at a stile beyond a cutting which goes across your line) and has some markers from forest walks before a surprisingly deep valley is encountered. The piers of the railway viaduct are still impressive. The forest is left by another stile; continue above a

INFORMATION

Distance: 16km (10 miles).

Map: Landranger 24.

Start and finish: The ferry pier at East Suisnish (GR 554342), reached by a 15-minute crossing from Sconser on the A87, 5km east of Sligachan. Hourly ferry service in summer but winter service still allows for this walk.

Terrain: Paths, sometimes wet, tracks and quiet roads. Cliffs: care needed.

Toilets and refreshments: Isle of Raasay Hotel (all year) 01478 660222; Outdoor Centre (summer months) 01478 660266.

The wild, white rose

Dun Caan from Kyle of Lochalsh

house (Glen Lodge) to reach the minor Inverarish–Fearns road, beyond which lies the ruin of the old powerhouse and the mine adit. The mining dates back to World War One. A forestry road with a Bailey bridge runs through beyond the felled woods, but it is probably as easy to cross the fence and walk on in the same line outside the fence and eventually dip steeply down to the Inverarish Burn.

Cross over and turn upstream to follow the burn nearly to its source: a winding, pleasant route even if a bit wet underfoot in places. The burn shrinks and wiggles, the ground to the right is scabby with slabs in places. A cairn on the skyline marks another view of your objective, with Loch na Mna (*loch of the woman*) close by. Above the loch, other cairns lead up left and along, on drier ground, with crags on the left. Keep right at a fork (left goes on to the crags) to pass along beside the loch then, with a bouldery scramble, reach and cross the inflow. There are superb views of the cliff-rimmed summit of Dun Caan from the lochside.

The loch had its 'beast' which preyed on women and children until a blacksmith – thereafter named Alastair na Beiste (*Alexander of the monster*) – lured it ashore by roasting a sow on the strand; the savoury smell was irresistible, the monster drew near and was slain by a red-hot spit. Boswell tells this story in his journal.

Head straight up the grassy slope ahead, aiming for where it meets the lower, left slope of Dun Caan.

Keeping left a bit, you can see the pass below (Bealach Ruadh) that runs through to Loch na Meilich with a path angling down to its end from the west side crags. This path starts off along the loch then turns to zigzag up to the summit of Dun Caan at 443m (1453 ft). Once met, simply follow the zigzag path to the top. There are a few markers and you should keep to the path to prevent erosion.

The summit is a magical spot, with a huge panorama both to Skye and the peaks of Torridon, Applecross and Kintail. The trig pillar is right on the cliff edge, so take care. To the south-west, the peculiar, tilted, green fields of Hallaig catch the eye: this was the site of a vanished crofting community, cleared of its inhabitants to make way for sheep. Notable scenery, including a fine, sea-cliff waterfall, requires exploration of this remote area another time, while the route up the east coast will challenge the hardy. The gneiss world of the north end (and Rona beyond) would need a long walk or cycle visit. Raasay is not to be visited just once – but make sure of good weather for Dun Caan. For his summit picnic, Boswell sat down to cold mutton, bread and cheese with brandy and punch.

Start back by descending the zigzag path to the end of Loch na Meilich (water board notice) and go up the angled path to the crags, beyond where there is a tiny lochan. The path heads off westwards over the moor then swings to the north (right) to make

Dun Caan

Symbol stone on Raasay

a long, steady descent to the island's 'main' road north near Balmeanach (lay-by/picnic table). Turn left along the tarmac – the road descends to a hollow then rises and swings right at a waterworks enclosure before regaining its south-westerly line. At an elbow where the road descends shorewards, keep straight ahead on another small tarred road, still on the south-westerly line of descent. There's a slight dip and rise and the youth hostel appears ahead. Turn off downwards on a track that leads to a gate and then angles down tightly above a house to gain the coast road at Oskaig.

The road leads south with fields running down to the sea and Ben Tianavaig bold across the sound. Scots pine, left, mark the start of pleasant forested walking, the sea below and Sgurr nan Gillean seen, unusually, through a frame of trees. Look out for an early (9th-century) symbol stone on the left. It has a decorated cross on the top and a tuning fork and crescent/'V' rod symbols. Shortly after there is the north drive of Raasay House (outdoor centre)

with a row of dogs' graves by the wall, with dates from 1871–1899.

Raasay

The centre offers welcome refreshments but, if aiming for a particular ferry, leave a good hour to reach the terminal. Behind the centre is the ruin of St Moluag's chapel (13th century) – unfortunately misspelt on the Landranger map. Exit by the south drive to the old farm buildings with a clock tower, which reputedly stopped working on the day 36 Raasay men wentto war in 1914. Only 14 returned. Continue along the road to the Isle of Raasay Hotel in its idyllic setting – as meals and refreshments are served all day, you may decide on a later ferry! The white church comes next then you drop down to Inverarish village. Turn right at the twin telephone boxes for the last coastal stretch. The Broadford and Sligachan hills look big and bold across the sound.

The Storr from Oskaig, Raasay

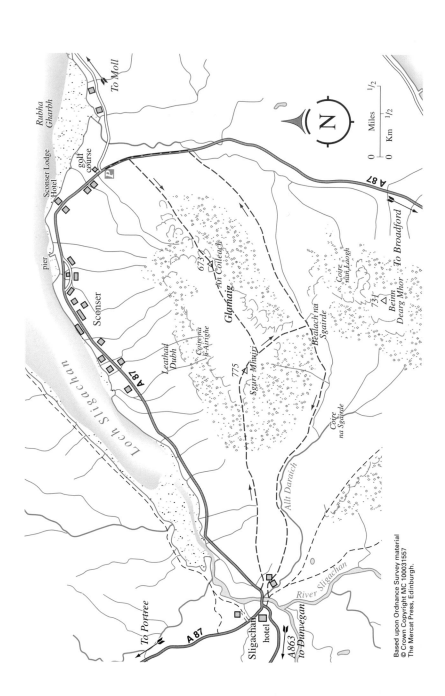

N

Miles ½ ½

Km ½ ½

0 0

To Moll

Rubha Gharbh

Sconser Lodge Hotel

golf course

P

pier

Sconser

A 87

Loch Sligachan

Leathad Dubh

Coire na h-Airighe

775

Sgùrr Mhairi

Glamaig

673 An Coileach

Bealach na Sgairde

Coire nan Laogh

731 Beinn Dearg Mhor

To Broadford

A 87

Coire na Sgairde

Allt Daraich

River Sligachan

To Portree

A 87

Sligachan hotel

A863 to Dunvegan

Based upon Ordnance Survey material
© Crown Copyright MC 100031557
The Mercat Press, Edinburgh.

GLAMAIG

The writer H.V. Morton arrived at Sligachan one wild night and next morning opened the blinds to find 'right in front . . . a tremendous Vesuvius called Glamaig shoot up into the air, a colossal cone, with ravines searing gigantic flanks'.

Glamaig is in this selection because it is one of the most outstanding summit viewpoints on Skye. It is not an easy walk from any direction, the slopes being very steep and with some minor crags and nasty screes.

There is no real technical difficulty but the ascent requires confidence and competence – and reliable weather. Have a look from below and if you have doubts, don't start. The classic view is from Sligachan, with Glamaig appearing as an imposing cone rising beyond the old packhorse bridge. In 1899, a barefoot Gurkha ran from the inn to the summit and back in 55 minutes – a fact that is more likely to depress than encourage.

Many will opt for the direct line up the hill, which can be seen and studied easily from below and presents no real problem other than unrelenting steepness with a ration of scree among the grass. Don't stray left (east), and take it steadily. Poles are a useful aid. This route has the *diretissima* advantage of landing you right on the summit, known as Sgurr Mhairi (*Mary's Peak*), 775m (2542 ft), named after a girl who was killed while searching for a lost cow.

A kinder and more varied route is to ascend by the north-east ridge over the minor summit of An Coileach. Most of the height is gained on very steep grass

INFORMATION

Distance: About 8km (5 miles), by either route.

Maps: Landranger 32, Outdoor Leisure Map 8, Harvey's Superwalker Skye.

Start and finish: Sligachan Hotel (GR 486298), or lay-by facing the Moll junction (GR 535318) on the A87 by Sconser golf course.

Terrain: Extremely steep slopes of grass and scree. Some scrambling.

Toilets & refreshments: Sligachan Hotel/café.

Blaven as seen from Glamaig

Walking along one of Glamaig's ridges

and there is some scrambly route-finding over An Coileach. Park vehicles in a lay-by just south of the Moll coastal road junction and walk along the A87 to where a fence heads straight up the hill. This marks the line, though the wise will zigzag rather than head straight up. The fence deteriorates to become just a succession of bare poles higher up. Traffic noise seems to echo loudly out of the glen below. Keep left of some crags until the main, highest, craggy area is reached, where it is best just to pick a route through to land on the fine summit of An Coileach, 673m (2190 ft), which translates as *The Cockerel*.

Beyond, the ridge on to Sgurr Mhairi is clear, the fence poles also dipping and rising on to the broader dome of the hill. The summit cairn lies off round the rim of the northern corrie and is an exceptional viewpoint by any standard. On a clear day (and the ascent should only be made on such) you can see the full length of the Outer Hebrides on one side and from Mull to Ullapool on the other. There are magical views towards Kintail, Raasay is clear and Ben Tianavaig and the Storr dominate the north. The rest of the Red Hills pile up, cone on cone, with jagged Blaven to one side and the sweep of the Black Cuillin on the other. This is what sets the song in the heart – and makes the toilsome ascent well worth the effort. There only remains the problem of descending!

Glamaig from the new bridge at Sligachan

You can return down either of the ascent lines described but, a traverse being more rewarding, one other regular line can be used: the Bealach na Sgairde, the gap leading on towards Beinn Dearg Mhor and Beinn Dearg Mheadonach. It appropriately translates as the *loose* or *scree* pass. Head back along the summit crest to find where the fence line turns sharply: this forms an arrowhead pointing the way to go down. The bealach soon comes into view, as do the slopes of scree, which aren't really avoidable.

If returning to Sligachan, the way back to the inn leads down by the attractive Allt Darach (*oak stream*) with its gorges and waterfalls; if returning to the Moll turn-off carpark, descend east and then flank along to circuit An Coileach's lower slopes on sheep tracks and reach the A87 where it bridges the river in the valley bottom. Beware of motorists: the short walk back along the A87 is the most dangerous bit of a Glamaig outing.

The present record (set in 1994) for the Glamaig Race, now an annual event, is 46 minutes and 2 seconds. In 1995, the event was won by a visiting Gurkha – but not barefoot this time.

Glamaig and Broadford Bay
from Mam Udal

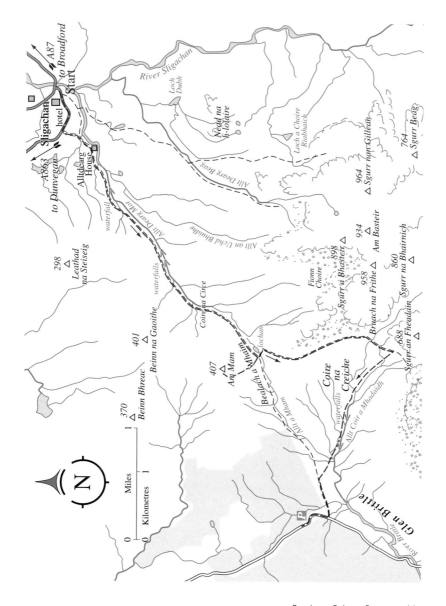

FROM SLIGACHAN TO GLENBRITTLE

Before the days of modern roads, this was a regular travellers' route to the then remote valley of Glenbrittle, so there is an element of history in taking this path from Sligachan. I regard myself as fortunate that this was how I first reached that glen nestling below the Black Cuillin. No walk gives a more varied and close view of these fabled mountains, and it is worth saving it for a settled dry spell, summer or winter. Rising to 344m (1120 ft) it is not a hard pass and Am Mam at 407m (1335 ft), the small hill just to the north, is worth climbing to extend the view into a typical Skye panorama.

The start lies 800m (half a mile) up from the inn on the Sligachan–Dunvegan A863 road where there are signs for a carpark and, unobtrusively, one saying 'Public footpath to Glenbrittle'. Walk up the drive until diverted round Alltdearg House and eventually climb the slopes parallel to the Allt Dearg Mor (*big red stream*). The going can be what the Scots call 'slaistery' (muddy and slimy) until the angle of ascent steepens. The burn has attractive falls and pools, and the scenery is on a grand scale, with the Pinnacle Ridge of Sgurr nan Gillean and the thrust of Sgurr a' Bhasteir dominating.

Eventually the angle eases for a wide hollow of open moorland, Coire na Circe, with Fionn Choire of Bruach na Frithe very obvious, due south – this is the easiest route up any Skye Munro and is a magnificent viewpoint. There is a confluence of burns here and not long after the path forks – the left branch heading for Bruach na Frithe. Take the right branch continuing towards the Bealach a' Mhaim, now showing ahead. Cairns begin to mark the route. Over on

INFORMATION

Distance: 11km (7 miles) linear.

Maps: Landranger 32, Outdoor Leisure Map 8, Harvey's Superwalker Skye.

Start: Sligachan Hotel (GR 486298).

Finish: Forest carpark above Glenbrittle, GR 424262.

Terrain: Rough path, rough, open hillsides, wet in places.

Toilets and refreshments: At the start, Sligachan Hotel.

Sgurr an Fheadain and the Allt Coire a' Mhadaidh

the left, the slope shows an area of gritty mounds split by a dark 'Y' of gorge and, at the col itself, there is a lochan, with the Glenbrittle hills now in view. There's a cairn by the outflow, which is a good spot to pause.

A 10-minute walk north leads to the top of Am Mam with a view over Loch Harport and Loch Bracadale to Macleod's Tables (two flat-topped hills) and a fine panorama of both Red and Black Cuillin.

Allt Coire a' Mhadaidh

A small path runs south-east from this col cairn past the lochan and on for the north-west ridge of Bruach na Frithe and, 100m beyond the outflow of the lochan, another path swings off left. This is the route to Coire na Creiche, which you take in preference to the direct continuation that simply goes on, passing a large cairn and dropping down to cross brown moorland and a forestry edge to reach the Glenbrittle road – a route which is also on the boggier side of slaistery.

Coire na Creiche is one of the Cuillin's showplace corries. It appears boldly before the motorist coming over from Carbost, its arms and crests in superb rock architecture and a pyramid (Sgurr an Fheadain, *peak of the pipes*) set in its heart. Fheadain is split from top to bottom by the Waterpipe Gully, which played an important part in early rock-climbing history. The pioneers came this way over the mam (Mhaim/*pass*) to climb Waterpipe Gully in 1895. The stream draining the vast cirque becomes the River Brittle and, after traversing into the heart of the corrie, the walk concludes by following the attractive stream down to join the road.

'Creiche' implies the corrie was once the hiding place for raided cattle, and it marks the site of the last battle (1601) between the Macleods and the Macdonalds: the two dominating clans on Skye. The clans had been niggling each other for years when Macdonald of Duntulm married the Macleod chief's sister. This was under a system of approval; if she did not suit, she could be returned after a year! She injured an eye, so Macdonald took the chance of sending her back – on a one-eyed pony, led by a one-eyed groom and with a one-eyed dog, an insult which could not be ignored.

The path from the Bealach a' Mhaim (shown on OS maps) flanks round under the flanks of Bruach na Frithe's north-west ridge, keeping to the drier slopes above the moorland. The jagged crest on the skyline ahead is many-topped

Looking down on Loch Sligachan from the Bealach a' Mhaim path

Sgurr a' Mhadaidh (*fox's peak*) and the bold prow enclosing the far side of the corrie is Sgurr Thuilm (pronounced 'hoolim', after a Gaelic hero, Tulm). Savour the rock-held fastness then follow the stream over the moors and down, keeping to the right bank. There are many attractive pools (which have become known as the Fairy Pools) and falls to tempt you to a paddle or a dip in high summer, midges permitting. Low down, one pool has an obvious submerged arch dividing it

The road descending into Glenbrittle is clear ahead – cut over towards it when the valley bottom is reached, merging with the direct path from the bealach and along the forest edge. There are attractive falls on the stream descending from the forest. In the forest, a short distance up the road (above the steep S-bend), there is a carpark/picnic area which is a good rendezvous if meeting arranged transport. The walk back directly to the Bealach a' Mhaim and down to Sligachan is an option too, of course, and gives splendid views to Glamaig and Loch Brittle as you descend.

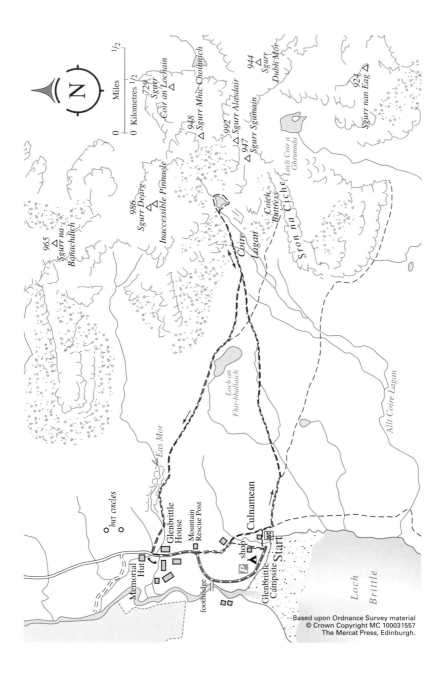

Based upon Ordnance Survey material
© Crown Copyright MC 100031557
The Mercat Press, Edinburgh.

COIRE LAGAN: THE CLIMBERS' VALHALLA

Coire Lagan is a memorably spectacular place which many walkers avoid, thinking it the preserve of the climber. Indeed, the surrounding peaks are Valhalla for climbers (weather and midges permitting), but the walk to Valhalla is open to all. This is a walk to indulge in mountain appreciation and perhaps see how the vertically minded perform.

The start is at the carpark at the head of Loch Brittle. Walk through the campsite (which has a shop) to cross a stile behind the white-painted toilet-block and head off up the Coire Lagan footpath, which has had remedial work to counter bad erosion. (Most Cuillin paths are on the wetter side of boggy.)

The stone-laid path climbs steadily. At the top of the first pull, a path forks right to cross a stream: it is heading round the coast or for the magnificent Coire a' Ghrundda, only accessible by scrambling. The Coire Lagan path runs parallel to, then crosses the stream and rises steadily towards the corrie portals between Sgurr Dearg (north) and Sron na Ciche (south). The going becomes rockier. Sron na Ciche presents a colossal cliff and a path splits off right towards it if a closer look is desired. Paths coming in from the left by Loch an Fhir-bhallaich (*loch of the spotted man*) come up from the Glenbrittle House/Memorial Hut area via the Eas Mor (a long-tailed waterfall) – this is the line of the recommended descent. A cairn marks the path fork, so note it for the way back.

The huge band of slabs right across the corrie is now

The huge cliffs of Sron na Ciche with the Cioch in the middle

near, and the path sneaks up the left (north) side of this. The final pull is over loose stones, scree or gabbro-rough slabs. It looks a barren world, yet it can produce carpets of thyme, starry saxifrage, alpine saw-wort, lady's alpine mantle, mountain everlasting, tormentil, bell heather and cross-leaved heath, to name a few, as vibrant in their way as names like Petronella, Crack of Doom, Integrity or Magic Casement to the climbing fraternity. Also note the large carpets of juniper.

Glaciated slabs by the loch in Coire Lagan

The lochan lies before you, filling the glacier-scoured corrie hollow with its cold, clear blueness and the warmer browns of weeds, dammed by slabs scarred by the passage of ice.

The heart of Coire Lagan is a textbook glaciated corrie, the slabs worn into boiler plates, and it is this that holds this lochan of clear water. It feels as if creation were only yesterday. Peaks of naked rock and scree torrents crowd round, including Sgurr Alasdair. At 993m (3257 ft), it is the highest peak in Skye, and was first climbed in 1873 by Alexander Nicolson, after whom it is named.

The Great Stone Shoot pours down from its crags with Sgurr Thearlaich and Sgurr Mhic Choinnich forming the back wall of Coire Lagan. The latter is named for the pioneering Skyeman John Mackenzie, an early guide and long-time partner and friend of Norman Collie – the extraordinary feature of the Cioch (Nose) was first noted, and climbed, by Collie. Its shadow, thrown across the Sron na Ciche cliffs, had alerted him to the then unknown feature.

Up to the left, more screes pour down between Mhic Choinnich and Sgurr Dearg, the latter crowned with a blade of rock still lovingly referred to as the Inaccessible Pinnacle: the most difficult of all Munros and second only to Alasdair in height at 986m (3234 ft). It was first ascended by Charles and Lawrence

Pilkington in 1880, Charles being Thearlaich in Gaelic. Skye is the only place in Britain where peaks are named after people like this. All this is country for the climber and scrambler rather than the walker, challenging as no other mountains can in the British Isles, and it requires some technical ability and skill in route-finding (magnetic rock renders the compass valueless),. The walker confronted with this majesty is likely to be torn between desire and despair.

Do make a circuit of the lochan and wander among the stranded rock whales that dam it. The view out and down is splendid. To the south stretches the great Sron na Ciche cliffs, and climbers will almost certainly be seen in action.

The Eas Mor

On leaving the inner corrie, keep to the right and take the cairned path that descends by Loch an Fhir-bhallaich to cross the moor to the stream issuing from the next corrie northwards. This plunges into a deep-cut gorge by the Eas Mor (*big fall*), which is a splendid spectacle. Follow the south bank down to a grassy saddle for the best view. Continue down and cross the stream at the water-supply intakes to reach the Glenbrittle road near the Memorial Hut and telephone box. Turn left to pass the sheepfold and Glenbrittle House (farm). When the road turns right (by the Mountain Rescue Post) keep straight on by tracks (and a gate to follow a meadow edge) to regain the campsite – or simply follow the road round to the carpark

The direct descent from Coire Lagan by the upward route gives pleasant views of the loch and its encircling arms. Glenbrittle campsite can appear idyllic in sunny evening light, but the truth is often different: the scene reminiscent of a battlefield, the joys of camping lost in some combination of rain, wind or midges, all of which, in Glenbrittle, can have stings in their tales. Keep Coire Lagan for a sunny summer afternoon.

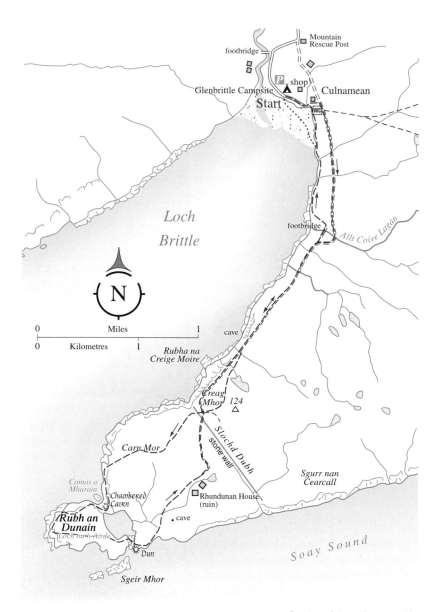

PREHISTORY AT RUBH' AN DUNAIN

Rubh' an Dunain (roo-an-doonan), *the Point of the Fort*, is the extremity on the south side of Loch Brittle. It gives a pleasant walk with no great heights to climb and with the inland mountain panorama balancing the outward view of the sea and islands. Most of the route is tracked, pathed or uses sheep tracks, but the going can be wet and wellies are quite in order.

Like all Skye walks it deserves a clear day to gain most from the views. While route details could be reduced to a sentence ('Walk to the point and return'), suggestions are made to make the most of the walk and to take in as many as possible of the prehistoric sites which are Rubh' an Dunain's speciality. Seals and otters may be seen and seabirds are common.

Arrive early: the carpark can be full in summer. The walk goes along the left side of Loch Brittle. Note the two 'hooks' of crag before Creag Mhor, which is the first objective. Walk through the campsite and over a stile behind the toilet block. Head straight up to gain an estate track and follow it southwards, a useful start to the day. If the big stream of the Allt Coire Lagan is too difficult to cross, there is a footbridge downstream (small falls). The rough track eventually becomes a path.

Nearing those juts of crag noted from the start there is a small burn to cross, after which the path splits, with the right branch continuing along the top of the cliffs (useful on the return walk) and the left rising to pass inland of the

INFORMATION

Distance: 14.5km (9 miles).

Maps: Landranger 32, Outdoor Leisure Map 8.

Start and finish: Carpark at the head of Loch Brittle (GR 410205).

Terrain: Moorland, some track, paths.

Toilets: Glen Brittle campsite.

Refreshments: None, but there is a store at the Glen Brittle campsite.

Creag Mhor and the Slochd Dubh wall

crags. Note the flat-topped, crag-rimmed lump of Creag Mhor. Walking on towards it, make sure of seeing the loch to the left, a fine, reflecting pool for the Cuillin. Creag Mhor is a first sampling of today's big views. Looking to the Cuillin (left to right), the first peak is Sgurr na Banachdich, followed by Sgurr Dearg, Sgurr Mhic Choinnich, Sgurr Alasdair, Sgurr nan Eag and Gars-bheinn, the last southern hook on the Cuillin crest. Seawards, Eigg, Rum and Canna are arrayed; a group (with hidden Muck) often called the 'Cocktail Islands'.

The Cuillin from Rubh' an Dunain

Head on to the next obvious small bump as this gives a clearer view of the ground ahead. The point is crossed here by a trough of valley, the Slochd Dubh (*Black Trench*), through which runs a stone wall. Note it well, for you cannot escape from the point without crossing this wall. With scores of flat-topped identical bumps, going astray is quite easy but should only be mildly inconvenient rather than worrying. Keep to the Loch Brittle side as you continue, aiming for the flat-pancake summit of Carn Mor, which overlooks the sea. Descend to cross the wall and then wiggle on through the lumps and bumps beyond. Carn Mor is a splendid viewpoint too.

Loch na h-Airde, nestling before the final point, comes into view from Carn Mor. A strange, long line of exposed rock heads off towards Camas a' Mhurain. Follow its line and enjoy the firm walking above the sea. A wall runs from this bay over to the loch: turn and follow it southwards and, on the last rise before the loch, look for an interesting chambered cairn which was excavated in 1932, revealing human remains and pottery. You can peer into the chamber from above to admire the work of many centuries ago. Ruins of old crofts abound all over the point.

Cross the wall and climb successive bumps to the last one, which has a cairn. The sea view is at its grandest here, with mainland peaks from Knoydart to Moidart in sight to the east and the Outer Hebrides to the west. Hecla and Beinn Mhor on South Uist show well. Soay lies to the east, close to Skye.

Continue round the point or cut across by ruined old houses to reach the outflow from the loch. Seaward, on the east side, the dry-stone walling of the dun (fort) is clear against the sky; 4,000-year-old workmanship that leaves you marvelling. Continuing round the coast, cut through the next gap, left, to reach a small valley which drains into the loch.

An unremarkable shallow cave (up right as you start up the valley) also contained signs of early inhabitants, including Iron Age smelting. A gable proves to be from quite a large house, Rhundunan, one end of which is rounded, and there are walled fields and gardens and other older ruins.

Start the homeward journey by heading on up from Rhundunan House then work leftwards (north) as paths/sheep tracks lead on; this will let you regain the Loch Brittle end of the Slochd Dubh gap with its wall. Drop down to cross this and turn left, seawards, rather than going over Creag Mhor again. A clear path is soon picked up, which wanders along rather splendidly between crags and sea cliffs, with the way ahead clear. The Cuillin can take on fiery colours as the sun sets, and Skye sunsets can be riotous, extravagant flourishes – definitely worth waiting for.

After the Allt Coire Lagan is reached, drop down to the bridge and follow a footpath along close to the shore. This reaches the campsite water tanks just above the toilet-block stile. It is also possible, if the tide is out, to drop on to the grey sands at the loch's head. A gate gives access back to track/carpark.

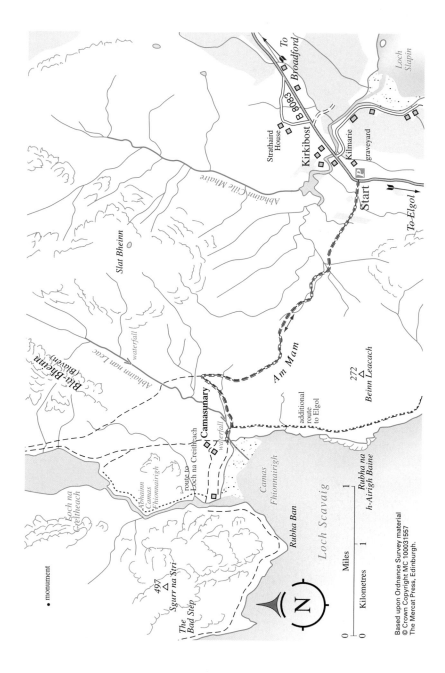

Loch Slapin

To Broadford

B 8083

Strathaird House

Kirkibost

Kilmarie

graveyard

Start

To Elgol

Abhainn Cille Mhaire

Slat Bheinn

waterfall

Am Mam

272
△
Beinn Leacach

Blà Bheinn
(Blaven)

Abhainn nan Leac

Camasunary

waterfall

additional route to Elgol

route to Loch na Creitheach

Loch na Creitheach

Abhainn Camas Fhionnairigh

Camas Fhionnairigh

Rubha na h-Airigh Bhaine

Rubha Ban

Loch Scavaig

monument

497
△
Sgurr na Stri

The Bad Step

N

Miles   1

Kilometres   1

0   0

Based upon Ordnance Survey material
© Crown Copyright MC 100031557
The Mercat Press, Edinburgh.

A VISIT TO CAMASUNARY

This is an easy walk with one of the finest near views of the Cuillin that walkers can enjoy. It leads to an idyllic setting, and is approached by an attractive drive through the Torrin and Strathaird country, now in the care of the John Muir Trust. Make the most of it, carry a picnic and swimming gear, and reserve the outing for a day when the weather matches the majesty of the setting. Leave nothing behind (except footprints) and collect nothing but memories. To many Skye enthusiasts this is holy ground. The easiest option is described, but a few supplementary suggestions are given for the more energetic. H.V. Morton wrote: 'I believe that Skye is the strangest place in the British Isles . . . one of Nature's supreme experiments in atmosphere.'

INFORMATION

Distance: 10km (6 miles)

Maps: Landranger 32, Outdoor Leisure Map 8, Harvey's Superwalker Skye.

Start and finish: Carpark on the B8083 Elgol road just past Kirkibost (GR 545172).

Terrain: Rough track.

Toilets and refreshments: Elgol only. Tea-room in summer. Shop.

The start is on the B8083 Broadford to Elgol road. After the road rounds the head of Loch Slapin and traverses under the serrated wall of Bla-Bheinn, also known as Blaven (Blaa-ven, *blue hill*), it climbs upwards, above forestry plantings, and then swoops down through Kirkibost and Kilmarie. As the road rises again, there is a large roadside carpark

Blaven from Torrin

The start of the Am Mam track

on the left with a gated track, stile and signs on the right. Park here. It can be busy in summer so arrive early.

One of the signs indicates the right of way to Camasunary and Sligachan and a plaque notes the 1968 attempt by the army to put a track in to Loch Coruisk, including blowing up the infamous Bad Step. Their track, which you follow to Camasunary, survives; the bridge they built was happily washed away and public outcry preserved the Bad Step and any further desecration. The track heads off clearly and gives easy walking.

The track passes a wood, dips and then winds up to a shallow col, Am Mam, before steadily descending the other side. Suddenly the view is revealed, 'one of the most dramatic surprise views on the island', with the green oasis of Camasunary below, black Sgurr na Stri fronting the Cuillin crests from Gars-bheinn to Pinnacle Ridge of Gillean (fine as alpine *aiguilles*) and Blaven running off up right. Southwards, the seascape is dominated by the island of Rum, with small Soay close to Skye. It is as perfectly composed and dramatically wild a view as you could imagine, and if you walk no further it will still set a song in the heart.

Camasunary from the Am Mam track

Right of Sgurr na Stri is a secretive stretch of water, Loch na Creitheach. The track, after some further traversing, puts in an elbow bend (where a path heads on for Loch na Creitheach and Glen Sligachan) and wiggles down to Camasunary. The bay is a gem with wide-green swards, two white buildings and sands rimming water, which can be startlingly blue under clear skies. Respect the peacefulness of the area. The far building is an open bothy, which is useful shelter if bad weather ambushes the visitor – though this is a corner really to be savoured on a settled, sunny, summer day. If wanting to explore a bit further, you can follow the river at the far (west) side of the bay up to Loch na Creitheach and back before finally heading 'home' over Am Mam to Kirkibost.

Another option, open to those happy with walking paths perched perilously over the sea, is to follow the coast southwards to the B8083 road-end hamlet of Elgol. The scenery is magnificent, but there are several places where the often-wet path runs high on cliff edges, which can be both intimidating and dangerous. You would also have to prearrange a lift or be prepared to walk 5km (or take the postbus) back along the road to Kirkibost.

Elgol is a road end of road ends as it is a renowned viewpoint for the Cuillin, and new carparks have been built near the tiny harbour. There is a seasonal

The Cuillin from Elgol

tea-room halfway up the steep road and a small general store at the top of the brae. The coast walk is signposted. Even if returning over the Am Mam, you should drive on the short distance to enjoy the special magic of Elgol. There are boat trips available from here too.

Famed Loch Coruisk is too enclosed to be visible on this walk, lying as it does behind Sgurr na Stri. The coastal path round to Coruisk is a demanding 3km extra, including the Bad Step, an awkward slab perched above the sea that has to be traversed by a crack line, so is not really an easy route from Camasunary. A boat trip to Coruisk from Elgol would be an enjoyable addition to the day. (Details from Tourist Offices or phone 01471 866244 *Bella Jane*, or 01471 866236 *The Nicola*.)

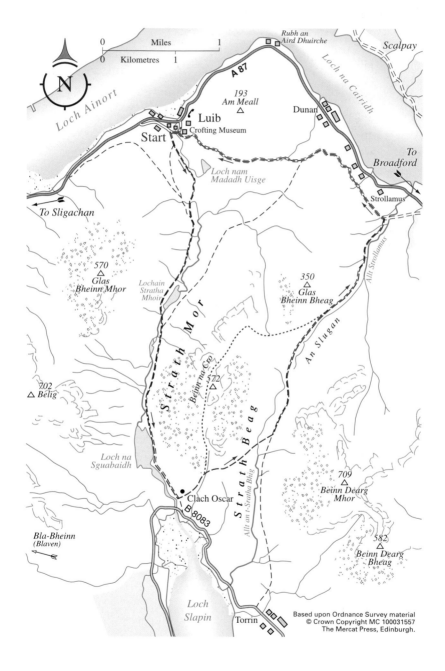

THE TWO GLENS

INFORMATION

Distance: 14km (9 miles), circular.

Maps: Landranger 32, Outdoor Leisure Map 8.

Start and finish: Luib (GR 565277), on the A87 between Broadford and Sligachan. Parking by the museum.

Terrain: Rough paths, very wet at times, track (old road) to finish.

Toilets and refreshments: Luib (Piper's Moon Coffee Shop in summer).

Opening hours: Luib Folk Museum 0900–1800, April–October.

his is a circular walk taking in two typical Highland glens: Strath Mor and Strath Beag (*big* and *little valleys*), set between high hills and giving constantly changing views. The watershed of Strath Mor is only about 35m. Given drastic global warming, Skye might be cut asunder along its length. Though both glens run roughly north–south, they link the east and west coasts of Skye. Strath Beag takes you to 180m, so the day's ascent total is modest.

Luib, a one-time crofting hamlet on the quiet shores of Loch Ainort, is the best starting point, lying roughly halfway between Broadford and Sligachan on the A87. Turn off this road at the sign by a telephone box and park between the coffee shop and the Crofting Museum – both of which are worth visiting at the end of the walk. Until the 1950s this was a picturesque crofting village of thatched cottages, long since rebuilt but retaining something of the atmosphere. The museum is the most accessible of several in Skye and gives a picture of life in centuries past.

Walk past the museum and over the bridge and turn left at the *second* gate (both gates have red

The folk museum at Luib

arrow markers). The path reaches the watershed in less than 500m. Strath Mor is a succession of lochs and streams and can be very boggy. After spates, it is worth avoiding or being prepared to divert from the route, with some back-tracking, if the main river cannot be

Lochain Stratha Mhoir on the Luib–Loch Slapin path

crossed south of the larger, northern Lochain Stratha Mhoir. The red screes of Glas Bheinn Mhor and Belig, last of the gabbro Cuillin, hem in the west, while Beinn na Cro lies eastwards, a long hogs-back between the straths. Prince Charlie came through this glen on his fugitive wanderings after the battle of Culloden in 1746. Keep to the path as not only are there hundreds of strange knolls but the strath has dangerous sinkholes.

The maps are not very accurate for switching sides south of big Lochain Stratha Mhoir, for the path happily continues on the west side of the valley and, once across, you join a clear traversing path on the east side. Cross at the first stream after the loch (cairn) and head up the heathery slopes for

about a hundred metres to find the path. The actual crossing from side to side has no clear path. A cairn will be spotted a little further on, if in doubt, and the path, once gained, is clear enough. In August, the lochs in the strath are graced with white water lilies and, earlier, the dainty heads of water lobelia.

The old route from the head of Loch Ainort came round the northern slopes of Glas Bheinn Mhor and through to Torrin to reach Broadford. Another path headed out of Strath Mor to Strollamus, once a large village, of which no sign remains: the Clearances removed the population. The A87 coast road was only constructed in 1923.

There's a sense of relief as Loch na Sguabaidh (*clean-swept loch*) is reached, assuming the shoreside path is not inundated. Note that the stream from the corrie south of Belig disappears on reaching the valley floor – opposite the outflow of the loch. High tides can leave seaweed well up the valley

Blaven seen from across
Loch Slapin

Bell heather nestling amongst the rocks

bottom. The Black Cuillin gabbro mountains continue on over Garbh-bheinn and Clach Glas to mighty Bla-Bheinn.

Bla-Bheinn (*the blue hill*, 928m/ 3044 ft) dominates the landscape of Loch Slapin, the only Munro (3000ft peak) not on the main ridge of the Black Cuillin, and a superlative viewpoint as a result. A Professor Nicol and the poet Algernon Swinburne first climbed it, from Loch Slapin, in 1857. Unlike Keats on Ben Nevis, Swinburne wrote no poem recording the visit. The John Muir Trust, to whom it was sold at a generous price by Jethro Tull band member Ian Anderson, now owns the hill and the Strathaird peninsula south to Elgol. The Trust is dedicated to safeguard and protect and, where appropriate, restore and renew our wilder, remoter landscapes both for their own sake and for those who live and work there – and for the benefit of future generations.

The Clach Oscar (*Oscar's Stone*) is a large boulder tossed here by one of the legendary Fianna (Oscar was the son of Ossian and the strongest of the band). It has split in two and split again and makes a perfect seat for a rest before you turn up the slope, left, to pass along outside the fenced pasture on the lower slopes of Beinn na Cro, at about the 110m level.

The Beinn Deargs from the Elgol road

Hold the height, or even gain a little, to round the south-east ridge of the hill into Strath Beag, dipping to cross the Allt an t-Sratha Bhig, on to the path which keeps up on the eastern flanks, whose slopes rise to Beinn Dearg Mhor. There are impressive views over Loch Slapin. Those keen on peak-bagging would find the route up seldom-climbed Beinn na Cro by its south ridge a rewarding 'extra'; it can be traversed down the north ridge to gain the broad watershed of Strath Beag.

The path up Strath Beag reaches about

180m (600 ft) then switches sides at the watershed. The initial descent is called An Slugan (*the gullet*), the path keeping close to the Allt Strollamus as it loses height. The island of Scalpay sprawls offshore (though it just looks like hillside ahead), one of the many 'islands which cling to Skye like children's hands on their mother's skirts'. The path descends to an old bridge on the ancient Broadford–Sligachan road and this is followed over and

Blaven from Oscar's Stone

down to Luib – a secretive hill route that passes south of the gentle cone of Am Meall, giving very easy walking and superb views to complete the day's circuit. Glamaig (Walk 8), the Red Hills, Glas Bheinn Mhor and all the day's hills are well arrayed as you cross the moor.

This old route is not a right of way, and walkers are asked to close gates and observe the Country Code. Loch nam Madadh Uisge (*loch of the water dog*) lies below you as you descend. Unfortunately, I have not been able to trace any story behind the evocative name. Loch na Sguabaidh in Strath Mor, on the other hand, was once inhabited by a choosy, maiden-abducting water horse (*each uisge* or kelpie) who only carried off beautiful lasses. The creature was eventually slain by a MacKinnon of Strath, south-west of Belig, in the Bealach na Beiste (*the beast's pass*) on the way to Loch na Creitheach.

The museum at Luib occupies one of the few surviving thatched houses, and as well as interesting furnishings there are displays concerning the wanderings of Bonnie Prince Charlie after Culloden, a story in which Skye, and Luib, played their part.

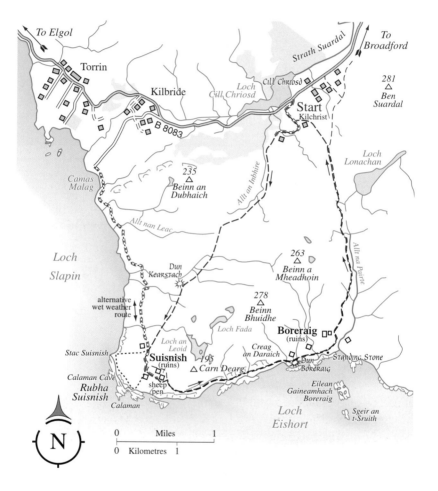

THE SUISNISH–BORERAIG COAST

This lonely, beautiful walk is tinged with sorrow, and anger, for the deserted hamlets you will see. The people were driven from their homes in the mid-19th century by Lord Macdonald's factors, who carried out cruel winter evictions regardless of the fate of children or the elderly.

Park off the road as soon as Loch Cill Chriosd is reached – not far past the historic church and graveyard. Cill Chriosd is *Christ's Church* but the site has been used since time immemorial. Much of the loch is covered in reeds and water lilies, so it has an unusually peaceful aspect.

From opposite the south-west corner of the loch, take a track which curves up and round a small spur and continues inland to a prominent ruin, part of the one-time village of Kilchrist. Though shown on OS maps, the path from there is either non-existent or difficult to follow. Swing right to follow the line of an old mossy wall, which reaches and descends by a burn. Note a row of trees along the line of another overgrown wall and cross to follow this towards other ruins. Looking uphill, aim to pass between an area of exposed limestone and a quarry where the path becomes clearer. It swings right as it climbs to cross the Allt an Inbhire (granite slabs) and continues through the gap in the hills beyond, where cairns on the skyline indicate the route. It is worth diverting on to the spur right of this saddle for the view and to see how the limestone is laid bare in extraordinary fashion. Beinn an Dubhaich to the north was also famed for its marble. Iona Abbey's altar used this Strath marble.

The head of the deep Allt nan Leac is crossed, then a wide, grassy, open valley, before a final, steeper

INFORMATION

Distance: 16km (10 miles) circular.

Maps: Landranger 32, Outdoor Leisure Map 8.

Start and finish: Roadside (B8083) by Loch Cill Chriosd, 4km from Broadford (GR 614205); alternatively from and back to Camas Malag (GR 583191).

Terrain: Paths, poor at times, and very wet in parts – there are alternative tracks and paths.

Toilets and refreshments: None. Nearest in Broadford, 4km.

Cill Chriosd

traverse. You must maintain the height. Below, the green-topped stony knoll is a prehistoric fort, Dun Kearstach, impressive in its isolation. The path becomes indistinct again but you should angle down steadily until the scattered ruins of the crofting township of Suisnish are reached. The house ruins, with their strips of land divided by walls, cover the point – Rubha Suisnish – and it is fenced off along its cliff edge as both cattle and sheep graze here.

A good estate road comes in from Kilbride (near Torrin), and if the weather turns bad this can make an easy escape route – from gaining the Torrin road it is only 2.5km back to the start of the walk. If the moorland crossings are likely to be wet, coming in and returning from Kilbride by this road is recommended. The coastal walk is enjoyable and there are interesting limestone features. Cars can be taken down to Camas Malag.

The sad sight of a semi-derelict house at Suisnish

When the track at Suisnish is reached, turn left to walk through the sad green place, passing one still-standing building with its row of ash trees. Alternatively, at all but high tide it is possible to descend to the shoreline at Stac Suisnish (not very imposing), walk round the point by the Calaman Cave and then climb up on a path, to reach the roofed but derelict building which may offer welcome shelter. The farm track ends at a sheep station. Most of the ruins are at a higher level so climb up the grassy fields to a central gate to gain the path traversing above the top fence. The path is clear all the way to Boreraig, another deserted village in the very different setting of a bay. Look out for seals and otters – and adders.

The path drops down to run along the shoreline with big bands of cliff above (Carn Dearg and Creag an Daraich) and thin falls descending to the coast.

The green lushness of Boreraig starts at a ruin, and seaward of this is another ancient promontory fort (*dun*). There are many ruins, often with fine stonework still showing. It is hard to imagine those living here being thrown out in the winter snows, their houses destroyed and left to survive or flee the country – all so the chief could run more profitable sheep on the land. Ironically, you may find cattle grazing at Boreraig today.

At the head of the last green, low-level field there is a small but obvious standing stone, and the return route begins there, heading up and inland above the Allt na Pairte. The going can be wet in places. Nearing the end, beyond Loch Lonachan, there is another area of limestone interest when the path drops to old marble-quarry workings. The easy option is to turn down the hillside here to reach the prominent building at Kilchrist where the beginning of the outward route is reversed back to the start. An interpretation board at Cill Chriosd tells the story of the local mining and the mineral railway line that once ran to Broadford.

On the Suisnish track

Heading back to Broadford, at the bend where the road twists up from the strath, there is a grassy bump on the left that marks the site of a chambered cairn. Across the valley, Beinn na Caillich (*hill of the old woman*) looks dramatic from here. The hill has a huge summit cairn where a princess of Norway was reputedly buried. This MacKinnon area of Strath was very much a buffer zone between the big aggressive clans of Macdonald and Macleod. Coire-chatachan (*corrie of the wild cat*), where Johnson and Boswell stayed, is supposedly where the last such animal in Skye was killed.

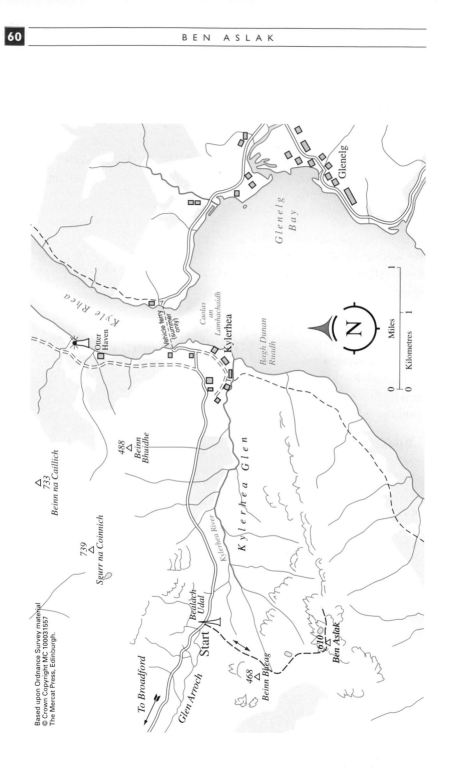

BEN ASLAK

Few hills of 610m (2000 ft) can offer such a short, easy ascent as this hill that stands above the Sound of Sleat; half the height is gained by motoring up to the Bealach Udal at 279m (950 ft). There is only limited off-road parking near the summit, so don't obstruct passing places.

Heading to Skye I find it difficult not to turn off over the spectacular Mam Ratagan pass to Glenelg and the Kyle Rhea ferry crossing on to the island, for the approach is both scenic and historic – and the ferry so much more fun than the toll bridge. Anciently, cattle being driven south to Lowland or even London markets *swam* across this narrow strait (*kyle/caol* = straits), presumably at slack tide, for the waters can go through like a river on the full ebb or flow. The inns for the ferry date to 1690. Boswell and Johnson found 'no meat, no milk, no bread, no eggs, no wine'!

On the Skye side, a road north leads to an otter haven with a viewing hide and with display boards. Heading inland up the Kylerhea Glen leads to the Bealach Udal with Ben Aslak over to the left, a road that seems to have borrowed a section of the Bealach na Ba in Applecross.

Set off south from the highest point of the road and just head up the slope, passing a couple of TV aerials and a bare rock slab as you make your way through tussock and heather. The going becomes easier with height gained when the grass and heather becomes short and extravagantly starred over with the flowers of tormentil in summer. A small stream leads up to the shallow col between Beinn Bheag and Ben Aslak, but the corner can be cut to pass a lochan and then ascend one of the grassy gullies breaking through the final rock bands – suddenly to discover an unexpected lochan at the summit.

INFORMATION

Distance: 5km (3 miles), circular.

Map: Landranger 33.

Start and finish: Top of the pass (Bealach Udal) between Kyle Rhea and Broadford (GR 753207).

Terrain: Pathless. Heather and grass slopes.

Toilets and refreshments: None.

Ferry: the Glenelg–Kyle Rhea ferry operates a summer-only service, April–September.

Foxgloves under the blue, summer sky

The summit lochan on Ben Aslak with Beinn Sgritheall beyond

This pool lies between two rival summits; the easterly has a cairn but the west is given the 610m spot height. There can be very little difference in the heights, so it's best to visit them both. The eastern offers a good view to the narrows (spot the ferry), the glens of Glenelg (Walk 18) and Beinn Sgritheall (dominating the start of Walk 17). The island in the Sound (with the lighthouse) is the setting of Gavin Maxwell's 'Camusfearna' of *Ring of Bright Water* fame. The western summit of this Ben with the C.S. Lewis-like name, Aslak, gives an incomparable view to Blaven, Glamaig (Walk 8) and the whole jagged crest of the Black Cuillin. Ben Aslak may be a small hill but its views are big and bountiful and it rests easy in an area of ancient traditions and lore.

The name Kyle Rhea could come from various sources, one of which is an old Fingalian legend. The Fianna dwelt near Glenelg and hunted on the hills roundabout, on both sides of the narrows. The slaughter of too many deer and the taking of too many salmon from the rivers over the years meant that the stocks became depleted and Fionn and his men were left lean and hungry, but for some unknown reason their wives remained fair and well-fed. One day Fionn left Conan to spy on the women, and he discovered they were eating hazel tops and washing in the water they had used to boil them. Conan, drawn by the smell of food, went forward and was welcomed and fed. As soon as he fell asleep, however, the women tied his hair to a hundred pigs and then yelled to start him awake. Once free, the infuriated warrior chased the women into a hut and put it to the torch. The Fianna saw the smoke from the Ben Aslak side and rushed to rescue their wives, leaping the waters with no difficulty except for

A tree-feller's sculpture with Ben Aslak and the Sound of Sleat beyond

Ben Aslak from Glenelg

one: Mac an Raeidhinn, who misjudged his leap and fell into the kyle, which was then named after him.

Sgurr na Coinnich (739m) and Beinn na Caillich (733m) lie north of the Bealach Udal and could offer more demanding ascents for experienced walkers if wanted. Both this Beinn na Caillich and the one above Broadford (which has a huge summit cairn) are reputedly the burial place of a Norwegian princess. The name means *hill of the old woman*, though!

Another of the Fianna legends is attached to this Beinn na Caillich. It is the reputed burial place of Grainne, the wife of Fionn, the Fianna leader. The Grey Magician turned her into a white bird and, despite searching for years, Fionn never found her.

Twelve years on the hounds were on a scent and the lead dog Bran, heading into a copse, turned suddenly to keep all at bay. Fionn found a wild boy who could only make the sounds of a deer. The warrior adopted him – to find this was his son by Grainne. They never found the mother, but on her death the magician relented to allow her son to take her body for burial on Beinn na Caillich where once she ran as a beautiful white hind. The boy had a tuft of hair on his brow from which he reputedly received his gift of poetry. His name was Ossian.

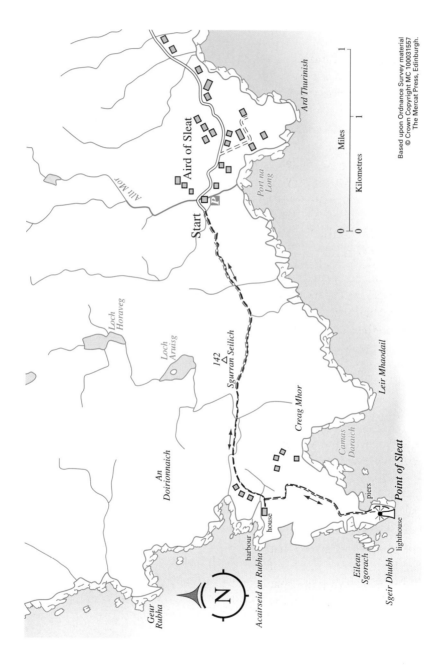

SKYE'S SOUTHERN END: THE POINT OF SLEAT

S leat (pronounced slate) with its lumpy moorland and lush, forested reaches on the sheltered sound facing the mainland is inescapably referred to as 'the garden of Skye' and has a great deal to offer the visitor. Most villages have a friendly hotel and there are many B&B places, bunkhouses and a youth hostel at Armadale, near the ferry to Mallaig (vehicles carried in summer, passengers all year). The Clan Donald Centre offers a major tourist attraction and is the base of a Countryside Ranger Service (tel 01471 844305/227), which organises local walks and other activities.

Those with cars should drive the minor circuit to the west coast with its spectacular views to the Cuillin from a whole string of crofting communities. These were established during the notorious Clearances when people were forced off better land to live in what was then basically wasteground. Ord, Tokavaig, Tarskavaig and Achnacloich form a unique spectacle. The road is narrow, often steep and tortuous and not for those of a nervous disposition.

After enjoying the lushness of the Sound of Sleat with its views to Beinn Sgritheall and Knoydart, the main road suddenly begins to twist and turn, rising well above the sea, edged by forestry planting, and finishing at the picturesque village of the Aird of Sleat. Radcliffe Barnett described this as a 'glamorous road that leads to the end of everything'. It stops by what was the old kirk, now converted into a whitewashed house. Park considerately.

The walk through to Acairseid an Rubha is on a rough farm

INFORMATION

Distance: 9km (5.5 miles).

Map: Landranger 32.

Start and finish: Turning/parking area at the road end at Aird of Sleat, 6km south of Armadale (GR 588007).

Terrain: Track and paths.

Toilets and refreshments: None (nearest Armadale, 6km).

Opening hours: Clan Donald Centre, Easter–October, daily 0930–1730.

Knoydart hills from Sleat

track and the extension to the lighthouse on the Point of Sleat is only a poor footpath, boggy in parts, with the typical ups and downs associated with Sleat. The atmosphere and views are of the very best.

The track winds upwards steadily initially and at a first summit there is a good view of the island of Eigg and the Rum Cuillin. The track dips and then rises again to the highest point, a small pass – from where Rum is the great eye-catcher – with the way ahead wiggling down towards a bay. The descent is steep at first then joins a burn in a hollow. This tumbles down by a small waterfall into a dark pool. The route bridges the burn a couple of times and then swings

away from the obvious bay, seen from above, to reach a house and the secretive bay, harbour and the double-cairned point of Acairseid an Rubha. The track keeps left of the house, with its sheltering trees and spring daffodils, to reach a gate at the top end of the harbour inlet.

Acairseid an Rubha

Through the gate, there is a slabby bridge over a small stream and then, immediately left, though not very obvious, is the start of the footpath to the lighthouse. You can find hours of pleasure in exploring the area of the harbour, with the challenge of the two cairns out on the far point. If heading for them, take the first opportunity of scrambling up on to the heather slopes above the quayside cottage where there are traces of path. Please respect the privacy and property of those living and working here. Issues decided in Westminster – even Edinburgh – feel remarkably remote if you live here.

The path on the map is token in character but, with perseverance, you can hardly miss the most southerly tip of Skye, as it is well indicated by its small, unmanned lighthouse. Start at the small bridge as mentioned above. The route goes up a rocky spur at first and then runs along parallel to the fence. Where the fence bends away sharply left the path swings to the right and then follows the crest of the peninsula to pass left of the barring brown hill (74m) ahead. Off right, there's a view down to a tiny bay. Look back, both to register the route and to note the many ruins of a once busy corner of Skye.

There is quite a distinctive 'gap' that suddenly opens up a charming view down to the bay of Camas Daraich. Swing right to follow along above the bay until, suddenly, there is the lighthouse in view – and a huge panorama of coast, sea and islands. The westernmost

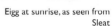

Eigg at sunrise, as seen from Sleat

point of Scotland (and Britain) runs out to the south, with Ardnamurchan lighthouse clear; Eigg and Rum dominate the nearer view; the Uists can be seen on the horizon; and, in clear conditions, Ben Nevis is recognisable. There is a steep descent (steps) to shore-level again, with the path exiting from a defile to round the intervening hillock on the west. The last hillock on which the lighthouse stands is reached by a causeway and then by steps and a clear path. There's a small hut on the way.

Return by the same route. The islet west of the point is Eilean Sgorach (*scallop island*), which is popular with cormorants. Watch and listen for divers with their 'loon' calls. This is too good a place to hurry away from, so bring a picnic and make the most of it.

At the time of writing much new fencing and work on improving the track was being undertaken and several herds of cattle were passed – a farming world which calls for admiration and respect. If you have to open any gates, make sure you close them securely behind you, and keep dogs on a lead at all times.

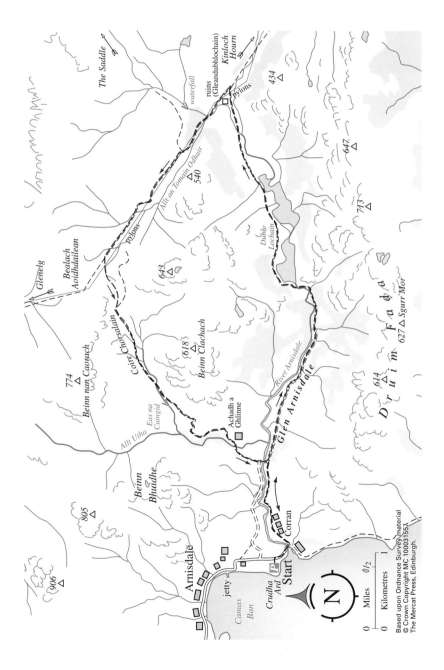

GLEN ARNISDALE CIRCUIT

T his walk takes you to one of the remotest corners of the Highlands, which gives it a very special atmosphere, quite apart from the dramatic scenery of the long approach drive. Even this remoteness depends on your perspective: when a visitor suggested to someone at Arnisdale that it was a long way from London, he got the response: 'Och, London is just as far away from here.'

The road runs high above the Sound of Sleat, with views across to Ben Aslak (Walk 15) and out to Rum. Much of the area has been planted with conifers, including the setting of Gavin Maxwell's *Ring of Bright Water*. Then the road swings round and down to Loch Hourn, with Knoydart's Beinn na Caillich (*old woman hill*) and Ladhar Bheinn (*hoof* or *claw hill*) across it. Loch Hourn, *loch of hell*, is an unhappy name for this extraordinary fjord. While a wandering road descends to its head (with difficulty), for many miles Loch Hourn has no road on this side and none at all on the Knoydart shore. You are indeed a long way from London, and not just in miles.

The last miles are dominated by Beinn Sgritheall (974m/3196 ft), a hill of great character and a mighty viewpoint, whose screes face the loch, a challenge for the mountaineer. The hamlet of Arnisdale lies round Camas Ban (*the fair bay*) and, not far beyond, the road ends at Corran where there is a carpark. The last house of this attractive hamlet is a small tea 'hut' – not to be missed.

While the sea was the ancient highway, many glens were familiar routes for those on foot, riding or driving cattle. Who knows

INFORMATION

Distance: 13km (8 miles).

Map: Landranger 33.

Start and finish: Corran, at the end of the road from Glenelg and Arnisdale (GR 849094).

Terrain: Mostly tracks and stalking paths but some rough mountain terrain. Careful navigation is needed on parts of this walk. If you are not competent with map and compass, do not attempt this walk in poor weather or mist. **Please do not take dogs on this walk.**

Toilets and refreshments: Sheena's Tea Hut, Corran (seasonal). Also does B&B (Mrs Nash: tel 01599 522336).

The River Arnisdale with Beinn Sgritheall in the distance

A garden in Corran abutting the River Arnisdale

how many cattle set off from Corran to the Lowland trysts – even to London? Going along Loch Hourn was too difficult, so they headed up Glen Arnisdale and through to Kinloch Hourn at the start of their long journey. You take the same track, signposted for Kinloch Hourn, just over the bridge and keeping to the riverside through successive gates (the track off right goes to a house) and over agricultural land where dogs are not welcomed. Pass one alder clump and then, after a gate, bear leftish to walk through a more extensive alder area. It may seem a bit confusing, but aim for the riverside.

At a wooden bridge, the path joins an estate track which winds along the valley bottom with Druim Fada (*the long hill*) sprawling to the south, its slopes covered in 'scrubby trees which bristle like the stubble of an old man's beard' (Butterfield). The gentle walking ends as you twist up to walk in the forest with the noisy river below. There are brutally steep zigzags up for a switch-backing traverse that brings the dammed Dubh Lochain (*black loch*) into view. The track plunges down and a bridge takes you across below the outflow waterfall to follow the north shores of the twin lochs, overlooked by Beinn

Clachach (*hill of the stony field*). That vehicles can make the climb is astonishing.

Ahead you will see a line of pylons that mark the onward route. The hill beyond them is The Saddle, much better known in the classic view down Glen Shiel. At a junction of rivers you can usually boulder-hop across, but note there is a bridge upstream. When the ruins come in sight ('Gleandubhlochain' on some OS maps), leave the track to curve round by the river and so join the pylons and a path coming up and over from Loch Hourn.

This heads north-west and up by a stream, which is then crossed (notable waterfall to the right), and the woody valley is followed for a while. The path, once clear of the trees, turns sharp right to wander off up into one of the corries south of The Saddle. Keep ahead, picking up the line of the intrusive pylons (taking power to Skye) which were blasted through this marvellous unspoilt country 'because there was nothing there'. Keep to the pylons' track, well above the Allt an Tomain Odhair, to reach the head of this wide glen. In 1981, a group re-enacted a Highland drove bringing cattle from Skye by this route to Kinloch Hourn. Telford, in

Lower Glen Arnisdale with Knoydart beyond

Eas na Cuingid

his surveying of the Highlands, proposed this route should be developed, but it never was.

The pylons march over the Bealach Aoidhdailean, but your route swings west below Beinn nan Caorach for Coire Chorsalain. Turn off at the fourth pylon down from the Bealach Aoidhdailean and work up on to the Beinn nan Caorach side of the pass to find and use a path which traverses, high and dry, along the north side of the glen. The pass is 416m (1365ft). There is a grand feel as you look into green Coire Chorsalain, with Beinn nan Caorach and Beinn Bhuide on one side, Beinn Clachach on the other and Knoydart's Beinn na Caillich far ahead, none of them Munros but no less impressive for that.

There is a lip and a second green 'flat' before the

easy angle dramatically changes as the burn dives over the Eas na Cuingid into the deep-set Allt Urha glen, a woody chasm seemingly miles below. A cairn marks a zigzag to avoid the gorge lip and another union of old path and Argocat track that traverses across to descend in a series of hairpin bends. There are superb views out to the Skye Cuillin and Corran nestling with Ladhar Bheinn, the westernmost mainland Munro, bold across Loch Hourn. A last twist lands you back in Glen Arnisdale where you cross a tubular bridge. The rusty-roofed house is Achadh a' Ghlinne (*the field of the glen*).

Cross the pasture to the bridge on the River Arnisdale where you rejoin the outward route back to Corran. The road route out goes by Arnisdale and Glenelg, and pretty Corran enjoys all the pleasures – and drawbacks – of a road so wrongly called 'dead-end'.

In 1836 the population was 600, and at times you could almost cross the loch on the decks of the herring fleet that was busy here.

There is an old story of an Ardnamurchan family who often brought their boat into Loch Hourn. They slept in the house of a local widow whose daughter fell in love with the son of the skipper, but he never seemed to notice her. At the end of one season, they set off for Ardnamurchan but gales kept driving them back all week. Suspecting the widow, the skipper visited a soothsayer and was given a rope with three knots and told the wind would be fair as long as the knots remained tied. Almost at the home jetty after a good sail, the skipper casually undid the last knot only for a gust to blow them out into the sound – and back to Loch Hourn. He forced his son to wed the widow's daughter, and thereafter the voyage home was trouble-free.

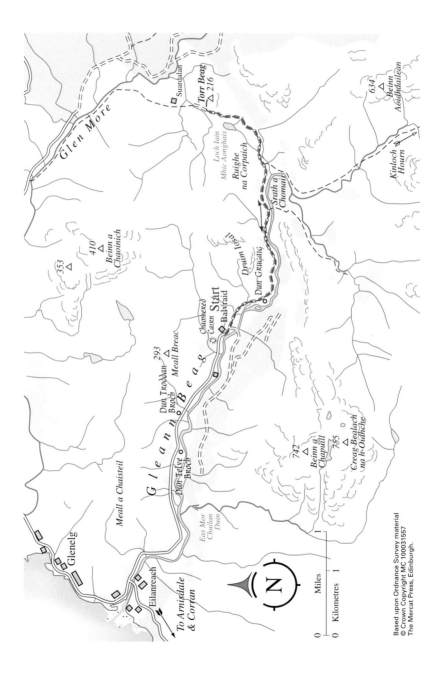

Glen More

Suardalan

Torr Beag
△ 216

634
○

Beinn
Aoidhdailean

Loch Iain
Mhic Aonghais

Ruighe
na Corpaich

Kinloch
Hourn

Srath a
Chomairt

353
△

410
△
Beinn a
Chaoinich

Druim Iosal

Dun Grugaig

G l e a n n   B e a g

Chaobried
Cairn Stàrt
Balvraid

Dun Troddan 293
Broch
Meall Breac

742
△
Beinn a
Chapuill

755
△

Creag-Bealach
na h-Oidhche

Meall a Chaisteil

Dun Telve
Broch

Eas Mor
Chuilan
Duin

Glenelg

Eilanreach

To Arnisdale
& Corran

N

Miles   0   1

Kilometres 0   1

Based upon Ordnance Survey material
© Crown Copyright MC 100031557
The Mercat Press, Edinburgh.

GLEN OF THE BROCHS

Glenelg is a very special place, which in times past was dominated by the easy access from the sea. Only with the building of the Bernera Barracks in 1722 and the later military road over Mam Ratagan was its hinterland breached. The ferry to Skye still operates (summer service only), and anyone using this book has good excuse to use the historic passage. Some of the stones for the barracks were pillaged from the nearby brochs, and it is perhaps these, as well as the delightful setting of Glenelg on the Sound of Sleat, which give Glenelg its special magic.

While it is possible to walk to the brochs, it is perhaps safer, on tarred roads, to drive there. Therefore the walk proper is described from Balvraid where the public road ends. The brochs are visited *en route*. The walk could be extended to finish in Glen More, rather than returning to Balvraid, but this would require some arrangement over transport.

Brochs are a mystery, which is part of their attraction. At a period that is very much a guess-timate (400 BC–AD 400) they emerged from nowhere – a great constructional advance on anything before. Then, just as inexplicably, they were no longer being built. They are obviously defensive, but who was the enemy? The Vikings are the likely answer: early raiders who came marauding before Norway became a real country with expansionist ideas. Gleann Beag has the two best-preserved brochs on the

Dun Telve – one of the Gleann Beag brochs

Eas Mor Chuil an Duin

Scottish mainland and only Mousa in Shetland is more complete.

Drive south from Glenelg and turn off up the minor road signposted for the brochs and 'Glenbeag' when the road swings in to the bridge over the Gleann Beag River. Keep an eye on the southern slopes for a waterfall, the Eas Mor Chuil an Duin, which can be very impressive when in spate, barely noticeable otherwise. Dun Telve, the first broch, lies among huge trees and can be seen, right, about 2.5km (1.5 miles) up the glen. Both brochs are in the care of Historic Scotland, so have interpretative notices and are well maintained. Basically, brochs are double-skinned circular buildings, shaped like cooling towers, with a small passage entrance. To a foe armed with swords and spears, they must have been impregnable. Dun Telve is interesting in having a barrier facing the entrance to make attack even more difficult. Mortar was not used in brochs; and the standard of work is astonishing. From Dun Telve, if you look up Gleann Beag, you can see the second broch, Dun Troddan, fascinatingly 'the same but different'.

Drive on to Balvraid, where the tarmac ends. If interested, walk back for a couple of minutes to see the chambered cairn marked on the map. It lies just over the fence on the last bit of open ground approaching Balvraid. There is plenty of parking space at Balvraid, but don't block any access.

Walking on, you leave the last of the farmland to twist up into the pass between Druim Iosal and the long eastern spur of Beinn a' Chapuill. Just over a stream, on the left and before the hill, there is a hut circle site and the big leaning stone has cup marks on its under surface. (Cup marks are circular indentations from millennia ago about which nobody knows anything – so speculation is rife. They appear throughout mainly western Britain and Europe, and even down to the Atlas Mountains of Morocco.)

Off right, after you pull up the brae, is some obvious

fortification walling. This is Dun Grugaig, which is an unusual half broch. Visit the site and you'll see why only half a defence wall was needed. It is thought to be of an earlier period than brochs proper, and is an atmospheric spot. The walk on is pleasant and will only improve with deciduous plantings across the clear-flowing river. There's a stretch of delightful birch, while alders hug the burn and there are rowan, hazel and willow – all native trees. At Strath a' Chomair, a route south-east is an old drovers' way through to Kinloch Hourn and eventually the Lowlands. Ruighe na Corpach (*ridge of the corpses*) indicates where coffins heading for home territory in Glenelg would be rested. Highlanders were often carried enormous distances to lie in home soil.

The track now swings northwards with the thrust of 216m (705 ft) Torr Beag ahead, the objective of the walk if returning to Balvraid and Gleann Beag. Torr Beag (*little knoll*) is also a prehistoric fort site and well worth a visit for it is a superb viewpoint. It is perhaps the best for Beinn Sgritheall (Sgriol), prince of the littoral Munros, seen over the lily loch

Torr Beag and the remote country found during this walk

of Iain Mhic Aonghais – the Gaelic for John MacInnes, who was drowned here. Legend has it he was using a waterhorse when ploughing nearby and the beast then plunged into the loch with him. The easy north-east slopes of Torr Beag still have the tumbled walls of prehistoric defences; the other slopes are steep and craggy enough not to need defences. Enjoy the view and then return by the same route.

The legends and stories of Glenelg (a rare place-name palindrome) have only been touched on. Artefacts and sites are still being discovered. In 1771, locals dug up a grave in which lay two giant skeletons. Could there be some truth behind the stories of the Fianna so concentrated in the area?

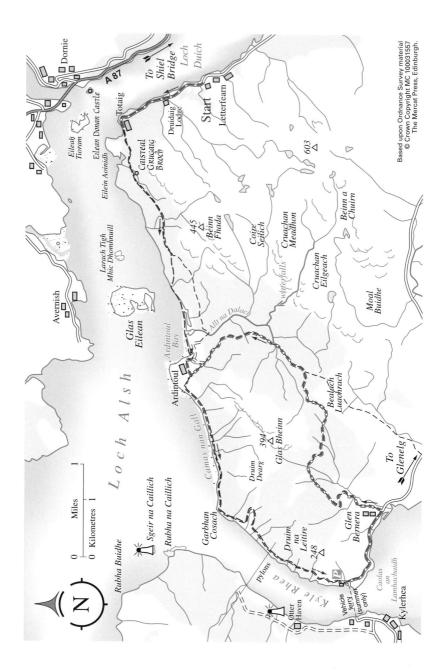

Based upon Ordnance Survey material
© Crown Copyright MC 100031557
The Mercat Press, Edinburgh.

A LOCH ALSH COASTAL WALK

This historical coastal walk, linking the Kylerhea–Skye ferry with the one-time Totaig–Dornie ferry across the mouth of Loch Duich, offers a varied and delightful outing. Allow plenty of time and carry food and drink for a day's walk if doing the complete route. If unable to arrange transport at both ends, a good circuit can be made from Kylerhea.

Parts of the Totaig–Ardintoul route are badly eroded, as gaps left in the tree plantings have been churned up by passing feet, but, as funds allow, remedial work will improve things. The route is described from east to west but can be walked equally well in the opposite direction.

Leave the A87 at Shiel Bridge on the Glenelg road and drive along the south shore of Loch Duich by Ratagan. At the scattered hamlet of Letterfearn simply park at the first chance, being careful not to block passing places or any access for locals. The road from Letterfearn to Totaig winds through magnificent woodland that is best seen on foot. Looking across Loch Duich, there's a view of Eilean Donan Castle.

Go through the gate beside the old ferry cottage and follow the good path round the bay with its tall larches then go through a gate in a deer fence with the path now shaded by conifers. The path crosses a burn and twists up to reach the impressive broch of Caisteal Grugaig, built of cyclopean blocks. It is extraordinary to find a 2000-year-old building using such massive stones.

Many people just visit the broch and return, and maybe they are wise, for the 'path' to Ardintoul is currently a mess, and were it not part of a greater whole, would hardly reward

INFORMATION

Distance: 10km (6 miles); circular alternative, 11.5km (7 miles).

Map: Landranger 33.

Start: Totaig/ Letterfearn on south shore of Loch Duich (or, circular alternative, Kylerhea ferry carpark).

Finish: Kylerhea ferry carpark, Glenelg.

Terrain: Paths, in places often very boggy. Remedial work should see the path much improved.

Toilets and refreshments: None. Nearest: Glenelg or Shiel Bridge.

The start of the walk from Totaig

The old ferry house at Kylerhea

the effort to cope with bogs and untrimmed trees. Head up steeply from the broch into the forest; pass a first nasty bit, then tackle a very steep ascent that sees the major uphill effort completed. Wind along on a poor path and, beyond a stream, turn up and then along – with more bog-bashing – to reach a sign pointing uphill 'To Ardintoul'. This route is best avoided. Ahead, none too clearly, another notice indicates 'Ardintoul: steep path' which is the preferred option. There may be better signing and route indication in place by the time you read this.

Take the steep path, which leads down to the edge of a craggy slope above the sea, to turn along through a conifer tunnel and debouch on to the shore by a gate facing Glas Eilean, an island of pancake flatness. Walk along the grass or shingle outside the wood. The Allt na Dalach is reached shortly after the high, alternative route escapes the jungle. There is no bridge, but its crossing would only be difficult after wet weather.

Keep close to the shoreline to reach Ardintoul Bay. Pass the markers for undersea cables and gain a track at a seaside cottage, follow it round the bay then turn inland to pass the attractive, big house (where James Hogg fell in love with the daughter of the house), and when the track swings left, turn right and walk down the fence to rejoin the shoreline. An Ardintoul Macrae introduced bagpipes to Nepal – and Gurkha regimental bands still use them today.

Some delightful walking follows. There's a glimpse of Dun Caan's sliced-off cone on Raasay (Walk 7), and beyond the bay's fish cages lie the Kyle Rhea narrows and Beinn na Caillich in Skye. Walk on along Camas nan Gall, with solid forest to the left, to the point of Garbhan Cosach where a gently rising path leads up into the woods. If coming the other way, it is essential to stay high by the forest fence to reach this point of easy descent – several dangerously steep traces of path drop to the shore earlier. The wood is largely birch and there are a few gullies to be crossed, but the restored path makes for enjoyable walking.

The next landmark is the huge pylon that takes the power line across Kyle Rhea (pronounced Kyle Ray). Walk under it then follow a track again out to the ferry carpark. This track undulates along pleasantly, leaving the forest more or less opposite the small, white light on the Skye shore and ending with a couple of gates. The route is signed at the ferry end if heading eastwards, but be sure of taking a left fork later to reach the big pylon.

Kyle Rhea

An equally good circular walk can be made by taking the coastal path to Ardintoul and then returning over the hill by a good track from Ardintoul to Glenelg.

Steep sections are surfaced. As soon as Loch Alsh drops out of sight, the feeling is entirely of mountains, with knobbly hills and secretive waterfalls rising above the forest level. From the top of the road, the Bealach Luachrach, a break on the right, makes it possible to climb Glas Bheinn, 394m (1293 ft) – an eagle-haunted height with a superb view down the Sound of Sleat. Return to the track by the same route as the hill is girded with cliffs and forest to the south and west.

The track twists determinedly down into Glen Bernera. Left of Ben Aslak (Walk 15) you can glimpse the jagged outline of the peaks of Rum, with Eigg left again. When the Glenelg–Kylerhea road is reached, there's about a mile (1.5km) walk along it back to the ferry.

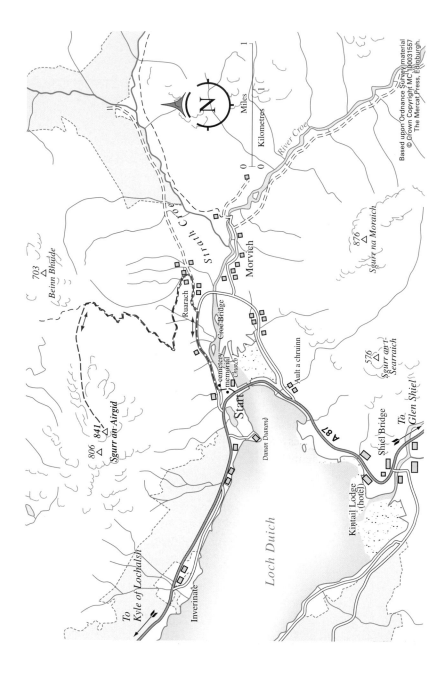

SGURR AN AIRGID, THE SILVER PEAK

INFORMATION

Distance: 10km (6 miles).

Maps: Landranger 33.

Start and finish: Lay-by on the A87, just north of the causeway (GR 946210).

Terrain: Stalking path and rough mountainside. Boots essential.

Toilets and refreshments: Ault a' chruinn, Shiel Bridge.

The writer Brenda Macrow described seeing Sgurr an Airgid from the west as a vast bulk with its rocks and streams shining in the sun, and suggested this was how it came by the name Sgurr an Airgid (*Silver Peak*) – the name is pronounced *errakit*. There is no record of mining.

The old road, signposted Morvich, which branches off the A87 north of the causeway, is the start of the walk, but there is no adequate parking on it, and the lay-by on the A87 just north of the causeway (below the memorial/cemetery/church ruin) should be used. There's a gate giving access to this historic site. The Clachan Duich burial ground spreads out from the old church which was dedicated to St Dubthach (*Duthac*) in AD 1050, though the site was in use some centuries earlier. The little lochan across the A87 is Loch nan Corp (*loch of the corpse*). The church was bombarded in the 1719 Jacobite fiasco.

Exit on to the old road where there is a cemetery parking area (you could park here at weekends), and walk along to a junction and find the road marked 'private'. Take this road for about 70m then head left, aiming roughly for a large solitary tree,

The old church of Clachan Duich below Sgurr an Airgid

The MacRae war memorial at the head of Loch Duich

and look for the rising line of a stalkers' path, which is the initial objective and can be seen slanting across the bracken slopes.

The path angles up then doubles back for a tortuous climb. You go through a gate in a deer fence (which keeps the beasts off the cultivated low ground) and the path leads on and eventually passes the western slopes of Beinn Bhuide. Abandon the path when the col to Sgurr an Airgid comes into view and traverse towards the peak. Note the area carefully to ensure that you can find the path again on descent. Airgid presents a green hollow facing east, held in rockier arms, which gives an easy ascent line, or you can keep more to the rocky crest which gives ever-expanding views over Kintail as you climb – all straightforward enough. A triangulation pillar marks the extensive summit area.

On Airgid, the hill of silver, you strike gold: it is a superlative viewpoint. You can see Ben Nevis, much of Kintail, Beinn Sgritheall, Rum and Eigg, the Cuillin of Skye, the big corries of Applecross, Torridon and Fannich ranges, as well as the Legoland world of Loch Duich.

Sgurr an Airgid over Loch Duich

Immediately north is a plateau, 'Lost World', covered in a host of lochans. Hugely present, too, is the end-on view of the Five Sisters of Kintail – Sgurr Fhuaràn at 1067m (3475 ft) being one of the steepest big hills in Scotland. W.H. Murray aptly wrote that 'in Kintail everything culminates. Nothing lacks. It is the epitome of the West Highland scene'.

Naturally, there is a legend about the Five Sisters. The story goes that once there were seven beautiful princesses.

Their father sheltered and helped two fair Irish princes who were driven ashore in a storm, and all seven girls fell in love with the visitors. Before departing, they asked for the hands of the two youngest princesses, promising that their five older, fairer, richer brothers would come to claim the other princesses. The king – and the princesses – were delighted. Alas, no other brothers ever came nor was word ever received of the two happy couples who sailed into the golden west. The five sisters refused all suitors, declaring they would rather 'wait for ever' for the promised princes. The grey magician ensured their vow by turning them into the five sweeping mountains known to all as the Five Sisters of Kintail.

Sgurr an Airgid from the Gates of Affric

North of the Five Sisters is the deep trench of Gleann Lichd where there is a spring, the Tobar an Tuirc (*the Well of the Boar*), the story of which has versions told all over Scotland (and Ireland) but seems very appropriate in this legend-haunted region. Here, by the well, is buried Diarmid, one of the fairest of the Fianna warrior band. The wife of Fionn (Fingal) put a spell (*geasan*) on Diarmid to carry her off on the very night of her wedding, which incensed Fionn.

He took his revenge with deadly cunning, arranging a great boar hunt to slay a notorious beast that had a poisoned spine on its back. The young Diarmid slew the boar but Fionn had him measure it from head to toe and then from toe to head until, in a careless moment, Diarmid brushed against the spine with his heel. As he lay dying he begged for water from a nearby well, but Fionn made sure it came too late.

Back to the present – back to earth – the descent is by the same route, any more direct way down being dangerously steep, rocky and having no helpful path.

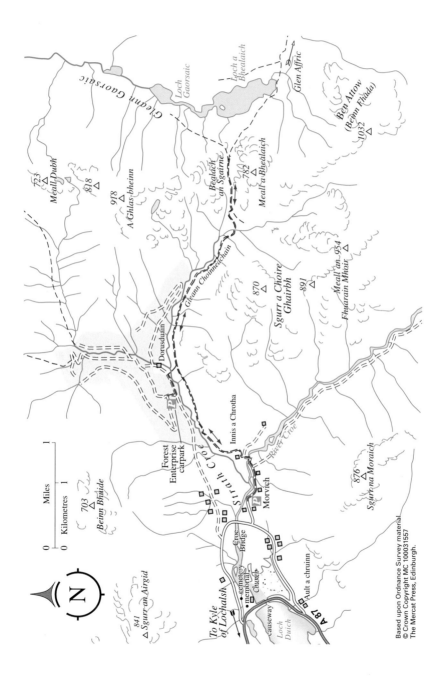

THE GATES OF AFFRIC

The Bealach an Sgairne (*Pass of Rumbling* or *Clattering Stones*) is the map name of the historic pass and is the objective of this walk. While it is virtually all on decent paths, the going is steep (from near sea-level to 530m/1700 ft), stony and sometimes wet. It should be treated as a proper mountain walk and kept for a clear day for both the character of the pass itself and the scenery and views.

There are two possible starting points, both off the old road round by Croe Bridge. From the south turn off the A87 where it is signposted for Ault a' chruinn (restaurant) and Morvich, the National Trust for Scotland's Kintail Countryside Centre/campsite. After 1.5km, turn off right to reach Morvich.

If coming from the north, just before the causeway is reached, turn left on to the old road, signposted Morvich. After 1.5km, take a small road on the left to its end at a Forest Enterprise carpark where the Glomach Falls walk starts – using this start makes the walk 4km shorter than starting at Morvich. From this carpark continue on the road (the tar soon stops) to go through a deer-fence gate, then angle down to the river where a long bridge leads across to the south bank to join the path from Morvich.

From Morvich, continue on the tarred road, passing the Gleann Lichd sign and the outdoor centre. The tarmac ends at a bridge, and the footpath is signposted for the Falls of Glomach. Another sign for the Falls of Glomach marks the junction with the route from the alternative start, which here joins the continuation along the glen.

The path soon swings round below the steepening slopes to start up Gleann Choinneachan (*Mossy Glen*) with the deep gullies flanking down A'Ghlas bheinn on the

INFORMATION

Distance: 11km (6.5 miles) circular from Morvich, 7km (4 miles) circular from Dorus-duain.

Map: Landranger 33.

Start and finish: National Trust for Scotland Kintail Countryside Centre at Morvich (GR 961210), or small forestry carpark west of Dorusduain (GR 978222).

Terrain: Steep mountain paths, rough and sometimes wet.

Toilets and refreshments: None *en route.* Ault a' chruinn, Shiel Bridge (cafés), Kintail Lodge Hotel.

The Gates of Affric from Gleann Choinneachan

other side of the glen. Birch scrub fills the glen bottom and there are some conifer plantings above. The path is clear enough although it is sometimes wet.

After a steady climb, the view opens out to the south with tumbling waters from the boisterous burns draining the corries of Ben Attow. Suddenly, the scenery is on a grand scale. Looking to the green slope beyond, you may pick out the zigzags indicating how your path continues. The zigzags pass an odd conical hump and, looking down, you realise just why the path has to climb. At a small cairn, a path branches off right. This is the standard route up Ben Attow but that sprawling giant (the name means *long mountain*) is only for those with considerable hill experience.

Loch a' Bhealaich from the Bealach an Sgairne

The mountain walls on either side begin to close impressively: to the south the bold grass and craggy thrust of Meall a' Bhealaich (*bump of the pass*), to the north the vertical strata of A'Ghlas bheinn's many crags. A final, deep slot leads to the col with its huge cairn. Few passes can equal it for sheer atmosphere. The spot has been well named The Gates of Affric.

This pass has been used for hundreds of years as a major east–west route to Kintail: armies, raiding clansmen and cattle thieves, refugees, drovers, packmen, have all used it. St Duthac crossed it in the 11th century, and, just down the east side, a well still bears his name (Loch Duich means *Duthac's loch*).

It is worth going on and descending a bit to where another path breaks off left at a small cairn. This twists up to a gap in the conical knolls where you find the viewpoint of viewpoints looking over Loch a' Bhealaich to whole clusters of hills and down Glen Affric to the high crest of Mullach Fraoch Coire. This path, not shown on the Landranger map, continues to Loch Gaorsaic, and

A' Ghlas-bheinn over Loch a' Bhealaich

a possible continuation for strong walkers would be to circuit the lochs and come up the main paths to the Bealach an Sgairne again. This takes you into remote country with the return/escape a hard *upward* haul, so is only advisable in settled weather and for confident walkers.

The descent from the Bealach an Sgairne is by the same route as the ascent, but this is no let-down as you are given a whole new set of views, including a very flattering vista of Sgurr an Airgid (Walk 20) and the causeway strung like a necklace across the silver neck of Loch Duich.

The area is full of legends. One tells how a Kintail shepherd was taking his ease by his fire when a score of cats entered and gathered round the peat glow. One by one they donned a cap, cried 'Hurrah for London!' – and vanished. The cap of the last fell off and the shepherd grabbed it, put it on and made the same cry. In a flash, he was in a London tavern where his ensuing wild night ended in his being hauled before a judge and condemned to hang for his sins. The rope was round his neck when his last wish, to wear his cap, was granted. Once it was on his head he shouted 'Hurrah for Kintail!' – and there he was, back home, with the noosed rope and the gibbet along with him. The rope he used on the thatch and the wood made the main beam for a new byre. They were aye-canny folk in Kintail.

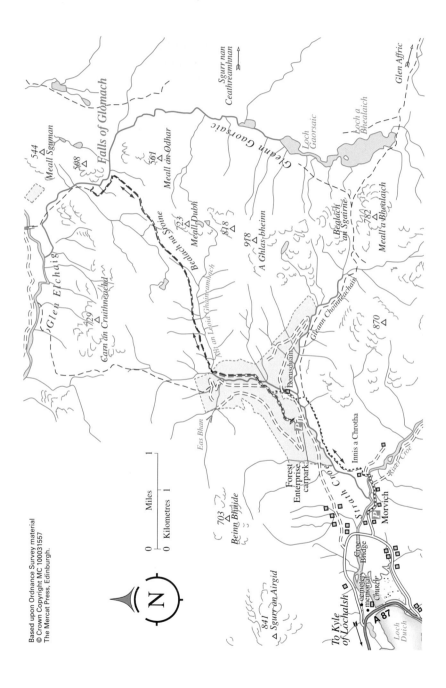

THE FALLS OF GLOMACH

This is a serious hill walk and should only be undertaken by the fit and confident. The route crosses a high pass to descend to the top of the falls so, on return, you are faced with an initial, stiff re-ascent to escape the back of beyond. In high summer, there is less water so the falls are not so dramatic, but in wet conditions, the dangers are considerably increased. Perfection is a visit on a sunny day just after a spell of wet weather, with a breeze to keep the midges at bay.

Turn off the A87 – just north of the causeway at the head of Loch Duich – on a small road, signposted for Morvich. Turn off again, *left*, where there is a notice saying 'Private Road' and arrowing the Falls of Glomach to the right. The warning of a height barrier is valid (2m/6'9") and, as there are 'humps' and potholes galore, you must drive slowly to the forestry carpark.

A sign at the carpark indicates the walkers' route: 'Glomach Falls, 4 miles'. As you walk up and along the valley, there are quite a few forks and junctions of forestry tracks, but no ambiguity as signs in each case indicate 'Glomach Falls'. There are views up Gleann Choinneachan (Walk 21) between the Munros of A' Ghlas-bheinn and Ben Attow.

A stream is crossed and the track traverses the hillside northwards to the end of the forest. The track doubles back upwards, but the walkers' continuation is straight on to a concrete-and-sleepers footbridge where the more demanding walking starts. Westwards, up a valley, there is a long, thin waterfall visible – though it needs plenty of precipitation to merit the name of *fair* or *white* fall, Eas Bhan.

The stream you cross by the bridge is the Allt an Leoid Ghaineamhach, which drains

INFORMATION

Distance: 12–15km (7.5–9.5 miles).

Map: Landranger 33.

Start and finish: Dorusduain forestry carpark (GR 978222), or NTS Kintail Countryside Centre, Morvich (GR 961210).

Terrain: Steep mountain paths, rough and sometimes wet. Cliffs at the falls: great care needed.

Toilets and refreshments: None *en route*: take food and drink with you. Nearest at Ault a' chruinn, Shiel Bridge (cafés), Kintail Lodge Hotel.

On the path to the Falls of Glomach

The green pleats of A' Ghlas-bheinn

the northern flanks of A' Ghlas-bheinn (*green hill*), the many runnels like pleats on the green skirt of the mountain. Initially, the path pulls up determinedly then traverses high along the glen, clear and giving easy walking as it undulates along. There is a feeling of expectancy as the world below has vanished and you become aware of the huge scale of the mountain country.

The path enters a narrow little valley, marked by many cairns, before reaching the summit: the Bealach na Sroine (*pass of the nose*) (510m/1600 ft). The cairns are a typical indication of an old 'coffin road', a route along which the dead were brought for burial in Kintail. At natural resting-places (like here, the top of a pass, with water available), the carriers would stop and add their stones of remembrance. Some people find it an atmospheric place.

The pre-war climber Frank Smythe, sitting just above the path and enjoying the scene, suddenly saw a group of ragged men, women and children straggle into the pass. Without warning a party of armed men leapt down on them and massacred the entire party before his eyes. Then everyone vanished. Explain that how you will.

The pass itself is barely noticed, for the path continues to traverse gently up and along. To the north-west, over moorland, the eye is caught by the rocky peak of Carn an Cruithneachd (729m) which perches dramatically over Glen Elchaig. There is a sprawl of hills to the north, and as you round the northern extremity of A'Ghlas bheinn (Meall Dubh), the bulk of Sgurr nan Ceathreamhnan fills the eastern view, a huge peak of peaks – which is sometimes jokingly called the Kangchenjunga of Scotland.

The path now begins its descent, first over gentle moorland slopes, then very steeply down a ridge crest into the valley draining to the falls, which are often heard before they are seen. Allt a' Ghlomaich means

Burn of the Chasm. Viewing the Falls is a rather frustrating experience as the gentle river suddenly drops over into such a deep cleft, and is surrounded by such rough, steep ground, that seeing them entire is impossible. There is a danger warning notice and this should be heeded. Dogs and children should be kept on leads! Vertigo sufferers should keep clear.

Having said that, if you are to see the falls you have to twist down a rocky footpath to a viewpoint. The situation is dramatic. The fall braids and plunges in its black cleft for something like 120m/370 feet (Niagara is only half as high), a height only surpassed by the Eas a' Chuill Aulinn in the far north-west of Scotland. Great care should be taken on this path, especially in wet conditions. There have been fatalities.

Top section of the Glomach Falls

The banks of the river are a favourite picnic spot, but it is well worth wandering 500m upstream to relax by (or in) pools and low falls, where there is a grand view back to Carn an Cruidhneachd. Return by the same route – it is worth noting the path's line on arrival in order to pick it up again for the hard upward escape.

There may be a temptation to link on through Gleann Gaorsaic to reach the Bealach an Sgairne (Gates of Affric, Walk 21), but this is a serious undertaking, giving a difficult day of about nine hours, and should be left for strong walkers well used to wild country. Many people feel a slight sense of unease, anyway, as the Falls really are in the back of beyond, far more so than many visitors have ever experienced before.

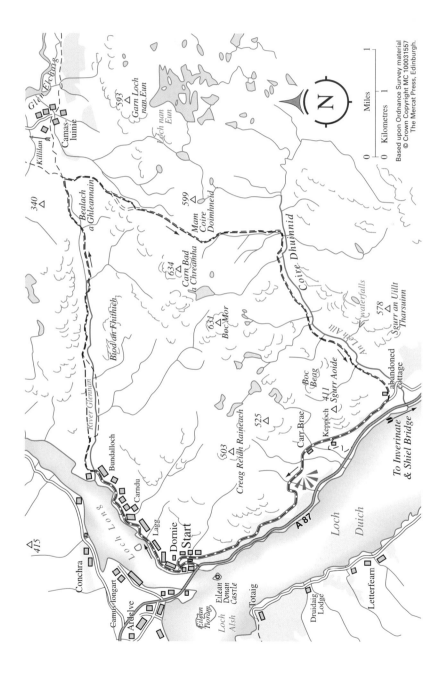

A DORNIE HILL CIRCUIT

INFORMATION

Distance: 19.5km (12 miles) or 14.5km (9 miles).

Map: Landranger 33.

Start and finish: Dornie (GR 882265) back to Dornie, or to Carr Brae if a shorter walk appeals.

Terrain: Rough, steep, wet paths in mountain terrain.

Toilets and refreshments: Dornie Inn, The Clachan (Dornie), shop at Carr Brae filling station.

Opening hours: Eilean Donan Castle, Easter–October, 1000–1700.

Dornie lies at the meeting of three lochs: Loch Long, Loch Duich and Loch Alsh. Duich comes from St Dubhthach or Duthac, an 11th-century saint and, with Eilean Donan Castle on the point, the area has had a notable history both spiritual and temporal. Dornie's setting is beautiful and this walk gives startling contrasts between gentle lochside and wild, mountain country. Though fairly short, it should be treated as a serious mountain day, for the going is often rough or wet (or both) and it has a real feeling of remoteness.

The last stage can be omitted if you make some arrangement with cars at both ends, and in warm weather this is no bad thing. The Carr Brae viewpoint could have one puffing up on a tarred road at the hottest part of the day. As the best of this section is the scenery, generally (and the superb sunsets), and the views down on to Eilean Donan Castle, this can quite happily be done by car. The rest is walking of quality.

From Dornie, walk along the minor Loch Long road, with its linked hamlets of Lagg, Carndu and Bundalloch where the road ends. Camas-longart and Conchra across the loch have a similar aspect and the reflected houses – 'clean-gleaming' –

The Dornie Bridge and distant Cuillin hills

golden seaweed and wizened hills make for a peaceful perfection.

At Bundalloch cross the bridge and turn right to start the riverside walk up the glen. Pass left of the sheepfold and, for about the first 3km (2 miles), keep to the north side of the River Glennan. (Maps show unnecessary crossings.) Wrens and stonechats are residents who favour rocks, screes and deep heather, probably more than human pedestrians. The going is both rough and wet in places.

In Glen Glennan

The glen narrows and screes fall right into the river; you can cross to traverse high on the south slopes or simply keep on the north bank in its deep 'V'. Either way you eventually criss-cross the stream.

You can break up again (right) into a secretive green corner and when the river is rejoined it is simply a trickle in the green bank. There is a spring from which it issues below a strange, smooth green apron held in the final 'V'. A last pull up (passing a welcome pool) leads to the pass, the Bealach a'Ghleannain, at about 230m (750 ft).

Ahead is a heathery bump. Leave the track to go right of this to gain another, much better path which heads determinedly up to the next pass, the Mam Coire Doimhneid, the day's high point at 525m (1720 ft). On joining the path, the tiny hamlet of Camas-luinie appears below in its rich Glen Elchaig setting. North lies Spidean Cointich and other bold summits. Killilan appears at the valley foot.

Killilan is connected with a St Fillan or Faolan,

The 'V'-slot of An Leth-allt
descending to Loch Duich

who may or may not be the same as the Perthshire
missionary saint, and a legend is attached to a
visit he made to France. Faolan had cut a hazel
staff by Loch Long and was told to return to
where he'd cut it and there capture a white snake
for a French physician. This he did by baiting a
pot with honey. On his return to France the
trophy was set over a fire and Faolan left to stoke
the fire with strict orders not to touch, but so
attracted was he by the bubbling pot he poked a
finger into one of the bubbles to pop it. From
this he received the gift of healing; the church
he founded at Killilan became famous in the west
and the Kintail people enjoyed great health.

The path keeps up the edge of a corrie, and you
should ignore a tracked section that joins the path
for a while. Higher up, the path bears left and
parallels the burn up the shallow hollow below the
col. The pass cannot be missed as there is a deer
fence and a gate. But, beyond, the path becomes
somewhat indistinct, so proceed with care.

Before descending, have a look at the map for
an odd feature: east, held in the gap between
two humps, is a loch with *two* outflows, a rarity.
One of them then flows into another lochan that
in turn has two outflows – perhaps a unique
feature in Scotland. As water flows both to Glen
Elchaig and to Loch Duich this chunk of Kintail
is 'a piece of land surrounded by water' – the
dictionary definition of an island!

The continuation keeps over to the right of the

A series of falls
on the An
Leth-allt

shallow (wet) hollow that begins the descent, then swings left to become a clear path again that descends the east bank of a stream which drops into a ravine. Fence and path turn right to cross the burn and begin the descent of Coire Dhuinnid, which is easy but wet in places, before the landscape becomes more dramatic. The path keeps high above the An Leth-allt (*the half burn*) which tumbles down in an endless string of falls and pools held within deep 'V's of green, with a glimpse of Loch Duich far below. Finally, you reach a deer fence and gate, with the path leading through an overgrown area of bracken to an abandoned cottage/sheepfold at the top of an S-bend on the Carr Brae road.

The walk back to Dornie turns right to pull up past Keppoch to the Carr Brae viewpoint. Then it drops down again to wind steadily along and down back to Dornie. There are splendid views down to Eilean Donan Castle and far views of Skye and the Cuillin. As mentioned earlier, this stretch of about 4.5km (3 miles) could be omitted if you

arranged for a car to be waiting on reaching the road. Parking is best down by the An Leth-allt bridge or off-road at the top of the S-bend. Whichever you choose, the views are memorable. It seems incredible that the fast shore road was only constructed in 1969.

Eilean Donan is probably the most photographed castle in the Highlands. It is actually a 1912–1932 reconstruction, the previous fort having been destroyed by a sea bombardment in 1719 during an abortive Jacobite rising. The first builders had a vitrified fort on the site (walls fused by applying great heat), but its real beginning was when Alexander III granted the site to a brave leader in the Battle of Largs (1263) when the Norse penetration – under Haco – was stopped. The leader was the founder of Clan Mackenzie. When the Mackenzies shifted their main residence to Brahan Castle (near Dingwall) the wild MacRaes became hereditary keepers and the great power in Kintail: 'Mackenzie's shirt of mail.' Both clans suffered for their devotion to the Stuart cause.

Eilean Donan castle

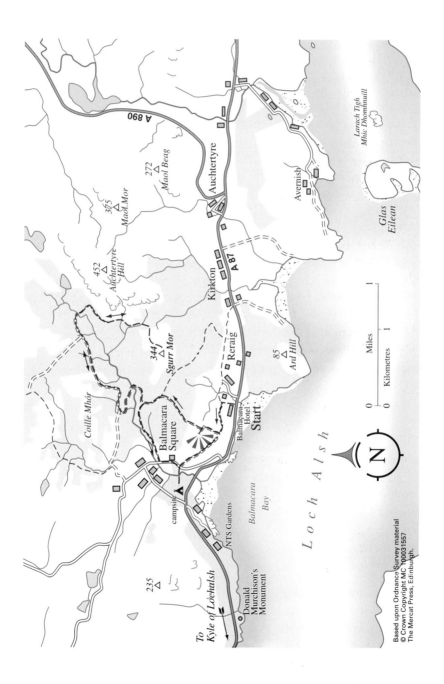

A 890

Maol Mor 375 △

Maol Beag 272 △

Auchtertyre Hill 452 △

Auchtertyre

A 87

Kirkton

Sgurr Mor 344 △

Coille Mhór

Reraig

Ard Hill 85 △

Balmacara Square

campsite

NTS Gardens

Balmacara Hotel

Start

Balmacara Bay

L o c h A l s h

Avernish

Glas Eilean

Larach Tigh Mhic Dhomhnuill

235 △

To Kyle of Lochalsh

Donald Murchison's Monument

N

Miles 0 — 1
Kilometres 0 — 1

BALMACARA AND SGURR MOR

INFORMATION

Distance: 11km (7 miles).

Map: Landranger 33.

Start and finish: Balmacara Hotel, Reraig on the A87 5km east from Kyle of Lochalsh (GR 814272).

Terrain: Reasonable tracks and paths.

Toilets and refreshments: Balmacara Hotel, Reraig.

Opening hours: Balmacara NTS woodland gardens: dawn to dusk all year (info kiosk in summer); Forest campsite (01599 566321).

Balmacara tends to be the collective name for the string of hamlets on the north shore of Loch Alsh as the A87 nears Kyle of Lochalsh. It is also the name of the National Trust for Scotland estate that occupies much of the area, whose mixture of farming, forestry and crofting makes a singularly attractive landscape. Sgurr Mor breaks above the trees to give a memorable view – and to reward the effort needed to gain its modest 344m (1118 ft).

The walk can be done equally easily from Reraig or the forestry campsite at Balmacara Square. Reraig is clearly signed on the A87. The Balmacara Hotel, a store/post office and filling station mark it out, and there is good parking on the seaward side of the road. The start is a gate at the gap between filling station and hotel, where there is a Forest Enterprise sign.

The path climbs up to a T-junction where you turn left (right goes to Kirkton) to pass a bench and gate pillars before reaching a crest where there is a sudden view down to Balmacara Bay, the Skye bridge and Skye hills. Inland looms Sgurr Mor, deceptively close. Turn up to the right on the metalled service track. Straight ahead leads down to the Balmacara Square road and the footpath into the campsite; coming up from which is another possible start, with the route right round the forest walk being marked by posts with a blue ring. The site is a gem and even has resident pine martens.

The old road winds up to a turning area and not far beyond is a view indicator. Features to note are the NTS woodland gardens, the monument on the point beyond (to Donald Murchison), the Skye bridge and the far Cuillin.

Sgurr Mor

Carr Brae viewpoint

Walk back to the turning place and turn left to reach the forest edge, just after passing under a line of power cables. The blue markers appear periodically and the path is clear as it meanders through the forest. A first picnic table gives a view to the Five Sisters and, later, there is another table at a line of beech trees. Continue on the path, which is joined by another (right), steadily losing height until a major fork. The blue markers go down left to complete the simple forest walk, and this continuation is described later. Right is the longer, harder route for Sgurr Mor, which is now described.

This drops to cross the Balmacara Burn; there is no bridge but crossing is rarely a problem. Beyond, the route continues to a gate on the forest edge. Just up the slope, a forestry track angles up to the right. Follow this for a long, steady tramp up the Balmacara glen. Auchtertyre Hill (452m) rather dominates the view but Sgurr Mor, with its knobbly crag, now lies over to the right. The long ascent, necessitated by the defensive plantings, allows for a pleasant circuitous walk.

After an open stretch, the track enters the forest again, through a kissing gate, and seems to be heading away from your objective. Keep straight on to the end of the track, above a stream – crossing shouldn't cause problems. Not far below, the stream drops over a cliff, and this dangerous ground should not be approached; keep to the path, the waterfall

Kyle Rhea from above
Balmacara

is clearly visible from Sgurr Mor. Take time to study the route ahead: a path running above the trees to a col from which a clear way up Sgurr Mor can be seen. It will not be so clear on the spot.

A path now leads round to traverse below craggy Auchtertyre Hill.

Not far from the stream, a path diverts left (cairn) but ignore this. Your path steadily descends and deteriorates and there are some boggy patches as it fights through the trees. The path almost dies on the col but a trace goes on, seemingly to a break, but as soon as the trees are reached turn sharp right on another small path and follow this till steep, open, heather slopes appear above. Climb up by the trees to the left and the path soon leads clearly to the summit – a fort-like setting with a magnificent panoramic view. The Five Sisters look grand and you have a good view over to Kyle Rhea, while an amazing array of Skye mountains are displayed.

To go down, unwind the route of ascent. Note the waterfall across in the far corner. There are quite different and rewarding – views on the descent. Re-enter the forest, cross the burn and reach the junction where the blue markers lead off downwards, thus picking up the forest walk again.

Moonrise from the Carr Brae viewpoint looking towards the head of Loch Duich

This path crosses the Balmacara Burn twice by bridges, then winds through birches and larches to descend steadily and escape out to fields. The edge is fenced off beside the stream (there are kissing gates) and the path ends at the Balmacara Square road (Forest Walk sign). Turn left, and just round the bend ahead, on the right, there is the signed route to the campsite start. Signs point across the road for the Kirkton and Reraig Viewpoint. Follow this track back up to rejoin the outward route, dropping down to the Balmacara Hotel.

Across from the store, a view indicator gives local information. The store sells local booklets, maps and guides, and the NTS woodland garden, not far away, is open all year.

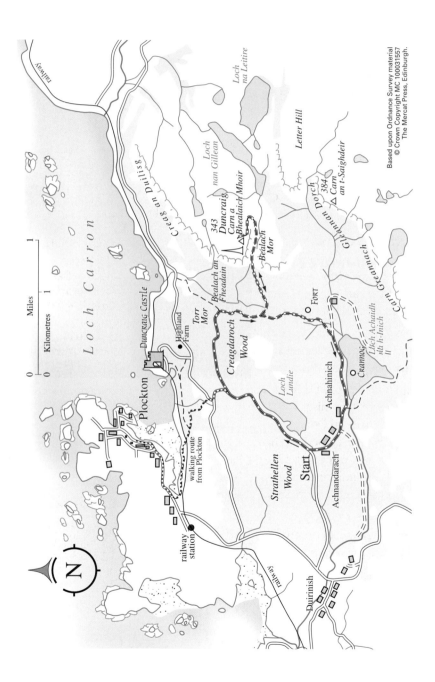

LOCHS AND CRAGS ABOVE PLOCKTON

Plockton must be one of the most attractive villages in the Highlands: palm trees grow along the shore and in every direction there is a backing of lush woodlands. Looking out over the bay, busy with marine activity in summer, you see the edifice of Duncraig Castle and, above it, the clenched knuckles of the Crags. On one of the highest, there stands a radio mast, the objective of this walk – a surprisingly easy one on minor roads and tracks.

Drive out of Plockton on the Duirinish to Kyle of Lochalsh road, which climbs steeply then edges the forest to Duirinish (*deer headland*), an attractive crofting hamlet. Both Duirinish and Plockton have accommodation, and it is an enchanting area to stay in.

Just before reaching Duirinish, if coming from Plockton, turn left on a small road signed for Achnandarach, Duncraig etc. (Coming from the south or Duirinish, it's the first road right after crossing the bridge at the top of the hamlet.) Follow this road to a junction where there is a bus shelter and a post-box and turn right for Achnandarach and Achnahinich. Park at the first available opportunity, but take care not to obstruct any access points.

Walk back to the junction and turn right, soon reaching the quiet waters of Loch Lundie in its forest setting. Not long after leaving the loch, a smaller, tarred

INFORMATION

Map: Landranger 24.

Distance: 10km (6 miles). From Plockton 13km (8 miles).

Start and finish: Achnandarach (GR803313). Follow signs for the Duirinish to Plockton road. Parking limited. The walk could be done equally well from Plockton.

Terrain: Minor roads and tracks (path if coming from Plockton).

Toilets and refreshments: Plockton has inns and a seasonal café.

The village of Plockton

The knobbly world behind
Duncraig Hill

road forks off right. Take this gently up through
Creagdaroch Wood, the *wood of the oak crags*,
though you won't see many oaks now.

The track leaves the forest at a cattle grid at the
Bealach an Fheadain, *the pass of the pipes*, a name
often given to spots where the wind can create
tuneful gales! Turn south to climb up along the
flank of a small glen. Craig, at its foot, has a
Highland farm open to the public, with everything
from ducks to llamas. At the top of the rise a track
breaks off, left, towards a gap below the crag with
the Duncraig relay mast on top. Follow this service
track to the mast: birches line the way up to a metal
gate and stile then the Bealach Mor (*big pass*) is
entered and the final steep ascent made from the
east.

Plockton and Duncraig Hill

The hill (343m, 1120 ft) is
more properly called Carn
a'Bhealaich Mhoir (*cairn of
the big pass*) and is not the
highest point in this world
of knobbles and water. The
purist may want to wander
up and down along paths
rimming the north-east to
reach the very highest

cairned bump, at about 358m. The seaward cliffs, Creag an Duilisg, should not be approached. Picking a return route should never be difficult with the mast as a guide. Use its access road for the only safe line of descent.

North are the corries of Applecross with the Bealach na Ba road running up into one; Torridon, Strathcarron and Killilan hills lead the eye round to the pleats of the Five Sisters; Sgritheall bulks boldly before Knoydart; while to the west, most of Skye seems to be on display.

Back at the maintenance road-end, turn left to a gate and descend rapidly through forest. After several hundred metres keep an eye open for a small cairn on the left bank which marks a short, steep path up to a notable prehistoric fort, which covers a surprisingly large area: walled where not defended by crag and with signs of mural chambers in the north wall. Sadly, having had trees felled in the interior, this has now been replanted – a crass disregard for one of the area's finest ancient sites.

The remains of the crannog on Loch Achaidh na h-Inich

Come out of the wood at a gate with Loch Achaidh na h-Inich (Achnahinich) ahead. Tucked in, back left, is the farm of the same name, at the foot of Gleann Dorch, *dark glen* – aptly named with its deep colours of heather and forest. A small islet in the loch is the site of a crannog, an artificial island dwelling – a system introduced in prehistoric times but not infrequently used much later. This site was occupied until the 17th century. Crannogs were constructed by driving a circle of piles into the loch bottom and filling the inside with stones. One has been reconstructed on Loch Tay in Perthshire and is open to the public.

There's another cattle grid as you leave the attractive lochside to wander through Ach-nahinich and Achnandarach, which are basically one long scattering of bungalows, linked by a dark tunnel of trees. Ach is *field,* inch is *island*, darach is *wood* (usually *oak*), so you can make out what the musical names mean.

If staying in Plockton, or willing to walk a bit more rather than drive to the start at Achnandarach, a pleasant extra route is available. A path for Duncraig is signposted between the High Sch ool and the main village area, and this leads round the sea bay and then passes under the railway line. After a rise it divides, the left-hand path going along to Duncraig Castle, the right winding up to meet the minor road to Achmore and Stromeferry. Turn right on this and then keep left where another road comes in on the right. You are now on the track coming from Achnandarach and Loch Lundie and can begin the circuit when you break off, first left, on the small road up to the heights.

Duncraig Castle and the crags

INDEX